when some one is asked
to write something, words
do not come easy. This is
one of those times:
- I'll be Maudlin - To a True
friend. A friendship I will
treasure for a life Time.
Maudlin perhaps - Trite + much to be sure
Allan

Rudolf Nureyev by David Hockney
1972

The Nureyev Image

Alexander Bland

OPTIMUM PUBLISHING COMPANY LIMITED

Quadrangle / The New York Times Book Co.

First published in the UK by Studio Vista,
a division of Cassell and Collier Macmillan
Publishers, Limited.

Simultaneously published in 1976 by
Optimum Publishing Company Limited
and
Quadrangle/The New York Times Book Co. Inc.

Trade distribution in Canada
Prentice-Hall of Canada, Ltd, Toronto

ISBN 0-88890-044-9

Library of Congress Catalog Card Number:
76–17509

International Standard Book Number:
0–8129–0664–0

Book design: Zena Flax
Jacket design: Sally Muir
Set in 12/14 pt Apollo
Filmset by Keyspools Limited, Golborne, Lancs
Printed and bound in Italy by A. Mondadori Editore, Verona

Contents

Acknowledgements

I should like to thank the many people who have helped in the compiling of this book. First the subject himself, who patiently went through some hundreds of photographs at moments snatched from his busy schedule, made available to me photographs from his own private collection, and also corrected several facts in the biographical chapter; the many photographers who responded with generosity and enthusiasm to my requests; Miss Josephine Hickey of Studio Vista for invaluable editorial advice; Mr Antony Tudor for making research in New York possible; Miss Bonnie Prandato for the loan of numerous precious pictures; Mr John Percival, on whose monograph on Nureyev I have depended for many dates and details; Mr David Hockney for permitting me to reproduce his drawing; and my wife for her active assistance and domestic endurance among an ocean of photographs.

Nureyev and the Camera

This book is primarily a photographic study of the art of Nureyev – to which his off-stage personality is an important appendage.

Like all dancers, Nureyev is fussy about photographs and films. He is right; eventually these records will be all that survive of his performances. Written descriptions can add details and suggest moods, artists can preserve something of the original impact and impression; but photographs have the character of factual evidence. It is they which form the historical image.

They are not reliable, of course. Photographs can mislead as much as any other description and any choice of them must be biased. A good deal can be learnt about a dancer by studying the pictures he prefers. There is an old story that, when glancing at a photograph of themselves, French dancers look first at the face, Russians at the arms, Americans at the legs and British at the feet. This may be a myth, but it illuminates the different national styles; and in the same way something of the aim and character of an individual dancer emerges in his likes and dislikes.

Nureyev is notably photogenic but notoriously difficult about being photographed. This seems to be due partly to a fear of anything which may disturb his concentration during a performance, or even a rehearsal; and partly to a hypercritical approach to the finished product. He will pass over without interest pictures which seem unexceptionable and pounce on others which are less perfect and less flattering.

He seems to seek out continually the image which expresses the feel of a movement rather than its appearance. He is mildly concerned with 'correctness' but much more insistent on the expression of vitality and emotion – the velocity or curve of a jump rather than its height, the plastic harmony of a position, what he calls 'juiciness' in a movement. Anything dry or artificial or insipid he detests. For this reason, action photographs have been preferred wherever possible to posed studies.

His own taste has doubtless left its stamp on this anthology; but it has by no means had the last word. The conjunction of a small set of pictures – or the choice of a single example – to suggest a whole performance injects another ingredient of commentary, and for this I am wholly responsible. Nureyev has approved the individual photographs, but the final selection and the manner in which they are presented, is entirely mine.

1975/76 — RUDOLF NUREYEV

perfs = X

	SEPTEMBER	OCTOBER	NOVEMBER	DECEMBER	JANUARY	FEBRUARY	
1	X Edinburgh Festival	Dutch Ballet Amsterdam	New York	Rehearse Covent Garden	Cov. Garden	Xm Palais des Sports	1
2	X		URIS – ABT	↓	X Manon		2
3	X			X M'chester	X Swan Lake	X Cancelled Rudi ill	3
4	X	Rehearse	X	X Cov. Gdn	X Cancelled		4
5	X			X ↓	X Romeo + Jul	X	5
6	X ↓		X		X R + J	X	6
7	Rehearse					X	7
8	Scottish Ballet		Xm	X HARTHA GRAHAM		Xm X	8
9	Glasgow	X	X	X SEASON NEW YORK			9
10		X		Xm	X ↓ R+J	X	10
11						X	11
12		Xm	X		PARIS T.V.	X	12
13	↓	X		Xm X	X	X	13
14		X	X		X	Xm ↓ X	14
15		X	X	X	X	Los Angeles	15
16	X MADRID		Xm ↓ X		X ↓	X ABT	16
17	X	X VIENNA	URIS – HUROK Xm	X	Paris – Palais		17
18	X	X ↓	X	X	des Sports	X	18
19	X	Xm	X X	X			19
20	X	X ZÜRICH	X	Xm	X		20
21	X ↓	X LUGANO	X		X PARIS T.V.	X	21
22	Rehearse	Xm	X X	X	X ↓	X	22
23	Dutch Ballet Amsterdam	X LAUSANNE	X	X	X Palais des Sp.	X	23
24		X BASEL		X	X	X	24
25		X BREGENZ	X	X	Xm X		25
26		X St. GALLEN	Xm	X			26
27		X GENEVA	X	X ↓	X		27
28		X			X	X	28
29		X HAGUE	X ↓		X	X ↓	29
30	↓				X		30
31				X Cov. Garden	X ↓		31

S. A. GORLINSKY LTD., 35 Dover Street, London WX1 4NJ England

Telephone : 01-493 9158   Cables : Gorlinsky London W.1

8

The Story

The Nureyev story begins like the traditional fairy tale: the youngest child of a poor family sets out alone into the great world, in pursuit of a treasure, fights monsters and giants and wins through to fame and fortune. The treasure was the chance to dance: he has found it, but it has not brought him the conventional by-product of retirement into domestic bliss. There remain many chapters still unwritten.

Nureyev is of asiatic Mongol stock. Both his father and his mother were Moslem Tartars, descended from the warriors who swept into Russia in the thirteenth and fourteenth centuries and left large colonies to the south. The family name was actually Fasli; through a clerical error Nureyev's grandfather was registered as Nuri. His father, Hamet Nureev ('son of Nuri'), was born in a small village near Ufa, in Bashkiria; his mother, Farida, was born in Kazan, and still speaks Tartar as well as Russian.

In 1938 Hamet Nureev was attached as political instructor to a regiment at Vladivostock on Russia's farthest Pacific coast. In March his pregnant wife set out with her three small daughters to join him; and as the train was rattling between the shore of Lake Baikal and the mountains of Mongolia the baby was born. Rudolf Hametovich Nureyev had made a characteristically dramatic and unorthodox entrance. It was 17 March 1938.

His sisters were, in order of age, Rosa, Lilia and Rezida. By the time he was three the family was living in Moscow. His father had been called up to the front when war broke out; not long afterwards the apartment block in which the family was living was damaged by bombing, and the mother and four children had to evacuate the city. They moved back to the Ural mountains, to their home province of Bashkiria, and settled in a little village called Tchichuna. Their new home was a tiny wooden house in the straggling, muddy village street. They had to share it with three other families, all five of them living in a single room together with a very old couple. The old people were Christians and the small boy was introduced to their faith by being persuaded to join in their prayers – an act of piety assumed for the standing reward of a morsel of cheese.

Life in this remote hamlet, always austere, was cruelly hard in these war years. The cold in winter was intense – the primitive sanitation froze solid – and food was scarce. Potatoes not eaten at once would be buried under the living room floor to protect them from frost. At Easter they would be exhumed, and Nureyev remembers sitting over the primus stove cutting out budding potato eyes with a knife.

It seemed an improvement when they were invited to move in with an uncle (a brother of Nureyev's father, who still called himself by the original name, Fasli) in the nearby town, Ufa. But living space was even tighter here than in the country; they all lived in one room together with another family, a claustrophobic situation which is not easily forgotten. Nureyev's only hint of a more spacious outside world was the family radio; he would listen to it by the hour, rejoicing especially when the death of some public figure changed the perpetual folk music to massive helpings of Beethoven or Tchaikovsky.

His first excursions to kindergarten only added to his trials. He was teased for his ragged clothes (sometimes, to his shame, cut down from his sisters' dresses) and feeble from malnutrition: he remembers the mortification of fainting in the classroom from hunger.

Then, on New Year's Day 1943, a few months before his sixth birthday, a new world opened. His mother had managed to buy a single ticket for a performance at the opera house and somehow the whole family contrived to squeeze into the theatre past the attendants. The five year old found himself watching his first ballet – a Bashkir legend called *The Song of the Cranes*. With an experienced ballerina (Nasretdinova) in the title role, it was probably quite well done; Ufa opera house was a large, well established theatre with a good reputation (Chaliapin had started there). To the small boy it seemed like a dream taking place in a palace. He decided then and there that he was going to be a dancer.

At the age of seven he moved from the kindergarten to school. With an exceptionally quick learning capacity and an almost photographic memory he found himself rising to the top of his class – a position which he was soon to lose as the result of another, and more important, temptation. Singing and dancing to the local Bashkir folk music was a regular part of the school curriculum, and became an obsession for the small Nureyev. He seized every chance to join in the displays put on for local festivities and hospitals, including the shows put on by the Young Pioneers, which offered a wide range of folk dances. His talent began to be noticed, and an elderly lady called Udeltsova who had once been a member of Diaghilev's corps de ballet offered to give him lessons twice a week in her children's classes. At eleven years of age he was performing his first classical exercises. Within a year he had made enough progress to be passed on to another teacher, a former soloist with the Leningrad Kirov Ballet, who organized amateur groups twice a week. His future course seemed set.

However, it was not to run without obstruction, now any more than later. His father wanted the boy to follow him into the army or at least to pursue his early academic successes in a professional career such as medicine or engineering. He was strongly opposed to his only son's adopting a career which even in Russia was eccentric for a man, and he sternly forbade all future dancing lessons. The boy was not to be deflected. For three years he kept up his resistance, sneaking away secretly to continue his lessons whenever he could, and in addition joining a Pioneer club where he took classes in folk dancing once a week. Inevitably his other schooling suffered. 'Nureyev works less and less,' his teachers complained. 'His behaviour is appalling . . . he jumps like a frog and that is about all he knows.

His determination was rewarded. When he was fifteen, a pianist attached to the opera got him the chance to appear with the professional company as part of the corps de ballet in a ballet called *Polish Ball*. After a few months he was appearing regularly, being paid for each performance and – most importantly – attending the professional ballet classes. At sixteen he was officially invited to join the company.

He refused. It was a typically reckless decision, but it was not unreasonable. He had his eye on a higher target, the school which had trained Pavlova and Nijinsky – the famous Maryinsky School of St Petersburg, now renamed the Vaganova Choreographic Institute, attached to the Kirov Ballet company of Leningrad. It was a wild but not an impossible dream and – as is the way in fairy stories – chance played into his hands.

Members of the company were chosen to represent the opera and the ballet at a festival of Bashkir art in Moscow. At the last minute the soloist failed to turn up at a performance; Nureyev (who had meanwhile failed his academic exams) boldly volunteered to take his place, in the solo from *The Song of the Cranes*. With only a few minutes to run through a dance which he had seen but never practised, he managed to impress the organizers enough to include him in the tour. Within a few weeks he was in Moscow.

Once again an obstacle appeared between him and his goal. During the strenuous rehearsals the over-keen and under-practised young aspirant strained a foot. It swelled up alarmingly and it looked as though his appearance before the formidable Moscow audience would have to be cancelled. However, he had recovered sufficiently by the day of the performance to take part, though not at full strength; moreover, he was auditioned afterwards by two teachers from the Bolshoi Ballet school, Gabovich and then the legendary Messerer. He was invited to join its eighth grade, one below the top class.

Once again he refused. He was determined to get to Leningrad. He bought a single ticket on a cheap economy train. It was packed and he could only find a place standing in the corridor; it stopped at every station and the journey took sixteen hours. The heat was intense but as they approached the city Nureyev noticed a black cloud hanging over it; eager to be prepared, he put on his overcoat and stood sweating as the train drew nearer and nearer. Finally when it arrived he found the cloud was smoke not rain. He made his way straight to the Kirov School – only to find that it was shut, and would not re-open for another week.

But again he was in luck. His old teacher from Ufa, Udeltsova, was in Leningrad and he was able to stay with her daughter, a psychiatrist. On

Nureyev as a student

24 August 1955 he was auditioned by a Kirov teacher, Costravitskaya. 'Young man,' she told him after the test, 'you will either become a brilliant dancer or a total failure – and most likely you'll be a failure.'

There were strong odds on her being right. When he entered the school the next day he was already seventeen, with only basic training at an age when he should normally be finishing his tuition. Moreover, though exceptionally quick at learning he was by no means an easy pupil. As a beginner he had to sleep in a dormitory with boys half his age, and to submit to the regulations designed for them. He was skinny, solitary and sharp-tongued; he resisted discipline, failed to conform and – worst of all – refused to join the political Komosol, as was expected of all keen students. Apart from his own talent there was one circumstance in his favour: the support of Alexander Pushkin, a teacher who combined inspired training with personal sympathy and understanding. He invited the highly-strung boy to stay with him and his wife; within three years Nureyev had passed through the whole

As a student in Leningrad with his teacher, Alexander Pushkin; another teacher, Natalia Komkova, and fellow-pupil Alla Sizova

La Bayadère

Corsaire - 1958

Nutcracker

Sleeping Beauty with Kurgapkina

Giselle with Shelest

Gayane

Beside a Leningrad canal

Pas de deux from *La Bayadère* with Lubov Voyschnis

The Leningrad years

course to emerge as the best pupil in the school. Even more impressive, he scored a big success in the all-Russia students' competition in Moscow against the strongest young dancers from the Kirov and the Bolshoi. He now had the chance to join either of these companies; without hesitation he chose the Kirov.

He met with immediate success, chosen almost at once by the company's leading ballerina, Natalia Dudinskaya, to partner her in *Laurençia*, and then taking leading roles with the other top dancers. There were serious problems, however. Soon after joining the company, he tore a ligament in his foot so seriously that a doctor recommended two years' rest. He took six weeks and returned to dance as fanatically as ever, travelling with the rest of the company to Vienna to appear in the International Youth Festival. At this time the thirty leading dancers at the Kirov were sharing only fifteen ballet performances a month, so that he could only expect a leading role about once in eight weeks. Between these performances he found himself being

With Irina Kolpakova in *Giselle*

With Natalia Dudinskaya in *Laurençia*

Photo Mike Davis

Above
As Solor in the full-length *La Bayadère*
at the Kirov Theatre

Right
Rehearsing *Giselle* in Leningrad

sent out on what he felt to be ignominious and damagingly tiring concert tours in East Germany and the Russian provinces. After complaining about one of these, he was told that he would be forbidden to dance outside Russia again.

For three years he danced with the Kirov, acquiring a following of enthusiastic fans. Notwithstanding the limited number of performances given by the company, he achieved a surprising number of roles during that time – *Laurençia, Don Quixote, Gayane, Giselle, La Bayadère, The Nutcracker, Swan Lake* and *The Sleeping Beauty* all offered him full-length parts, and he also appeared in many shorter numbers such as the *pas de deux* from *Chopiniana (Les Sylphides)* and scenes from *The Red Poppy* and *Taras Bulba*. He danced with a great variety of partners, including Dudinskaya, Alla Shelest, Alla Sizova, Irina Kolpakova, Olga Moiseyeva, Alla Osipienko, Xenia Ter-Stepanova, Ninel Kurgapkina and Inna Zubkovskaya. He was busy and successful, but he was not happy. With official opposition mounting and his own dissatisfactions increasing, an eventual collision seemed inevitable, with consequences which were easy to predict.

It was time for luck to intervene and it duly did. Early in 1961 the Kirov company was booked to appear in Paris and in London. As he had foreseen, Nureyev was not chosen to go; but only a few weeks before the date of departure the leading dancer of the company, Konstantin Sergeyev, was suddenly informed by the management that he was to be replaced in some of his ballets. There was only one possible substitute –

17

As the Prince in *The Sleeping Beauty* at the Kirov Theatre

With Alla Sizova in *Le Corsaire*

Photo Michael Peto

Nureyev. On 11 May he set out – officially publicized as 'one of the most exciting dancers to emerge for a decade' – for Paris and London.

As the Prince in the Kirov *Sleeping Beauty* at the Paris Opéra

He did not dance on the opening night – the first-ever appearance of the Kirov in Paris – but when he did, the effect was sensational. He was given extra performances (not always announced in the programme), and promised opening appearances in London. This dramatic acclaim, coupled with a now defiant disregard for company regulations about staying out late and mixing with foreigners, was more than his superiors could stand. There must have been some agitated communication with Leningrad and Moscow and when the dancers assembled at Le Bourget airport to board the plane for London on Saturday 17 June he was called aside and told that he was to return at once to Moscow for a special performance in the Kremlin, and to re-join the company later. Nureyev guessed that this was the point of no return; once back in Russia he would never be given another chance. Glancing around he saw that two stalwart men, whom he had previously noticed talking to the Director, were standing by the exit. It was a moment for a quick decision. He said a hurried goodbye to the rest of the company. Then he moved over quietly to two French policemen who were standing in the hall, told them he wished to stay in France and asked for their protection. He was led into a waiting room and sat there while the forty-five minutes for reflection obligatory under French law passed in anxious silence. Within an hour he was on his way back to Paris. Now he really was on his own.

Photo Garofalo

First thoughts in Paris after the Kirov Company had left

Photo Serge Lido

This quick curtain on his life in Russia marked the end of the first act in Nureyev's career. The next episode, set against a very different background, with an entirely new set of characters acting in a strange idiom to an unfamiliar tempo, was to offer an even greater test to the central figure, as well as wider opportunities.

With what can now be seen as characteristic practicality and speed he plunged wholeheartedly into the nearest ballet activity. On 23 June, the very night the Kirov Ballet opened its season at Covent Garden with *The Sleeping Beauty*, he made his first appearance with a Western company, partnering Nina Vyroubova in the same ballet. He had embarked on a six-month season with the international Grand Ballet du Marquis de Cuevas.

Nureyev joins the de Cuevas Ballet, Paris

Rehearsing for his first performance with a Western company, in *The Sleeping Beauty* with Nina Vyroubova

Photo Daniel Camus

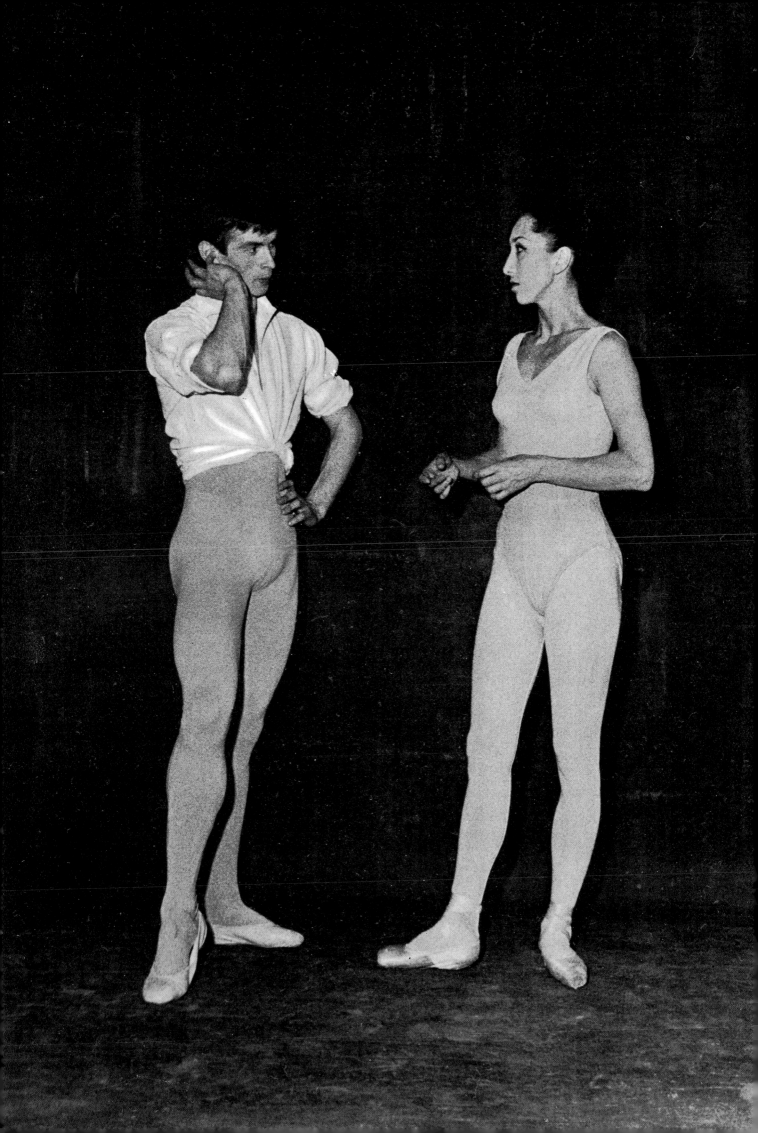

He had already met the director of the company, Raymundo de Larrain, who had designed the fantastic production in which he found himself. The working conditions (he alternated the roles of the Prince and the Bluebird, a switch he was accustomed to in Russia but not for such frequent performances) and the atmosphere of this touring company were very new to him, and at first he was pursued by journalists and harrassed by the Soviet authorities. De Larrain could guard him in his own apartment by day, but there were some demonstrations during performances and sometimes an upsetting telephone call would come through from his family or from Pushkin in Russia just before he was due to go on stage. He toured round France and Italy for a year – learning the hard way the conditions and methods of ballet in the West without making any ambitious experiments.

He did, though, make one noteworthy excursion, to Copenhagen. Here were a teacher, Vera Volkova, who had studied in Leningrad, and also a dancer whom he greatly admired (from a brief film he had seen in Russia), Erik Bruhn. The great Danish artist – ten years older than Nureyev – was to prove a close and faithful friend who not only helped him with his work but could give him advice and information about the strange new dance scene into which he had launched himself.

Copenhagen also saw the beginning of another significant relationship. One morning the telephone rang in Volkova's flat and a voice came through from London. It was Margot Fonteyn asking her whether the young Russian would be right for a charity matinee Fonteyn was organizing. Volkova was enthusiastic – he was 'something of a genius – he has the nostrils'. What was more, Nureyev was in the flat. He accepted Fonteyn's invitation immediately; there would be no fee for the still impecunious stranger – just his expenses; a newspaper had offered to pay for his ticket in return for an interview. To avoid unwelcome publicity he arrived unheralded and passed under the name of a Polish dancer called Jasman who had originally been scheduled to appear (for some time afterwards he was known to his London friends as 'Jazz'). He and Fonteyn struck up an instant understanding ('he is the first Russian I have seen laugh,' she remarked delightedly). He met Ninette de Valois, Director of the Royal Ballet, and found her Irish temperament immediately responsive to his Russian one; and Frederick Ashton agreed to write a short solo for him for the gala. A vital connection with the Royal Ballet had been sealed within a few days.

After a few weeks with the de Cuevas company he returned to London for the gala. His short, stormy solo, *Poème Tragique* to a piece by Scriabin (seen in retrospect, it must have been almost as much Nureyev as Ashton), and a *pas de deux* with Rosella Hightower received an ovation – such passionate abandon was something new for London audiences; even Fonteyn, who had rejected the proposal that she should dance with him at the gala on the grounds that she would be too old for him, was convinced, and a collaboration between the two became just a question of time.

In the meantime he danced out the remainder of his contract with the

Photo Georg Paul Günsberg

A day in the country

de Cuevas company and even embarked on a short trial piece of independent enterprise. He, Bruhn, Hightower and Sonia Arova made up a concert programme and gave some performances, first in Cannes, then in Paris – the first try-out for what were later to become many ventures outside regular companies. It led to his first engagement in America. On the last night in Paris Bruhn hurt his foot and was unable to dance the Bournonville *pas de deux* from *The Flower Festival at Genzano*. Nureyev promptly learned it and added it to his own contributions; what was more he undertook to replace Bruhn in a New York television performance of the work a few days later. It was an echo of the withdrawal of Sergeyev from the Kirov's Paris season: once more luck, talent and enterprise had carried him on to a new battlefield.

Meanwhile Nureyev's debut with Fonteyn had been fixed – not

25

without difficulties. Conservative opinion had been deeply shocked at the idea of a dancer 'deserting' his company and some, misunderstanding his motivation, prophesied a quick decline into popular entertainment. Others were understandably nervous at the prospect of inserting this clearly obstreperous character and very un-British style of dancing into the Royal Ballet. Many experienced voices were raised in opposition. Even Sir David Webster (who had been woken from his first sleep after returning from his company's Russian tour by an urgent voice begging him to book the young runaway) may have had his doubts. But de Valois had none. Justifiably confident in the solidity of her company, she declared that a new and different talent could prove nothing but a stimulus. Her unstinting determination played a big role in launching Nureyev's career in the West and she was to have the satisfaction of seeing her opponents confounded.

His first appearance was in *Giselle*, in the same production which he had watched on his first night in Britain. It was not a ballet in which Fonteyn had ever been especially successful and on that evening she had not been on top form. But Nureyev, though puzzled by a style of

Outside the Brooklyn Academy after his debut in New York

Photo Martha Swope

dancing and miming very different from what he was used to, at once appreciated her quality, and on this first appearance together it was evident that an instinctive artistic understanding made them perfect partners. What quickly became a legendary double-act was under way.

His attachment to the Royal Ballet was now a matter of course (he became a regular guest-artist – as a foreigner the question of his joining the company did not arise); soon afterwards he set out to show his work in New York. He did not repeat the London pattern by joining a major local company in a large theatre; he appeared on stage in an out-of-town theatre for only a few minutes, dancing the *Don Quixote pas de deux* with Arova in a programme mounted by the Chicago Opera Ballet company in Brooklyn. But by now he was a celebrity and almost every ballet notable was in the theatre. He received an enthusiastic reception and America was added to his now international audience.

The pattern of his life over the next decade had been set, and it was to vary only in detail. It involved regular appearances with the Royal Ballet both in London and on foreign tours, coupled with frequent shorter engagements with other companies. The publication of an

With Sol Hurok, the Russian-born New York impresario who managed his American appearances

Photo Vartoogian

Photo Ardan

With Fonteyn and Karsavina (former star of Diaghilev's Ballets Russes and partner of Nijinsky) at Karsavina's eightieth birthday party in London

autobiography which had been compiled by a French agency, mainly from a number of interviews (as soon as he became established he was anxious to stop publication, but it was too late), marked the definitive break with beginnings which he relegated firmly into the past. 'Never look back,' he declared. 'That way you fall down stairs.' He was determined to rid himself of the image of the rags-to-riches wonderboy who 'leaped to freedom'. He wanted to work as a dancer and be judged as a dancer, an artist for whom the present and the future were more important than the past.

By the end of 1962, when he had been in the West for a year, he had danced in France and Germany, Britain and America and Italy (with the Kirov he had already been to Austria, Egypt and the Lebanon). He had even visited Australia, flying out to see Bruhn after an injury had set his career in doubt. With the money he saved he had acquired a home on the French riviera. In London he lived in a series of furnished flats until – later – he was to move into a rambling house near Richmond Park. He travelled in an ever tighter routine from country to country, widening his experience and steadily enlarging his repertoire.

Like the schedule of any committed artist, an account of his engagements and dancing achievements over these years reads like a glamorous grocery list. It is only a close look at it which reveals a combination of pace, stamina, quantity, quality and variation which is quite extraordinary. The number of performances he has contrived to fit into every week, every month, year after year certainly constitutes a record. This unremitting rhythm has also entailed switching constantly

With Erik Bruhn off the French riviera

Photo Serge Lido

Photo Arthur Todd

With American choreographer José
Limon and dancer Igor Youskevitch

Travelling outfit

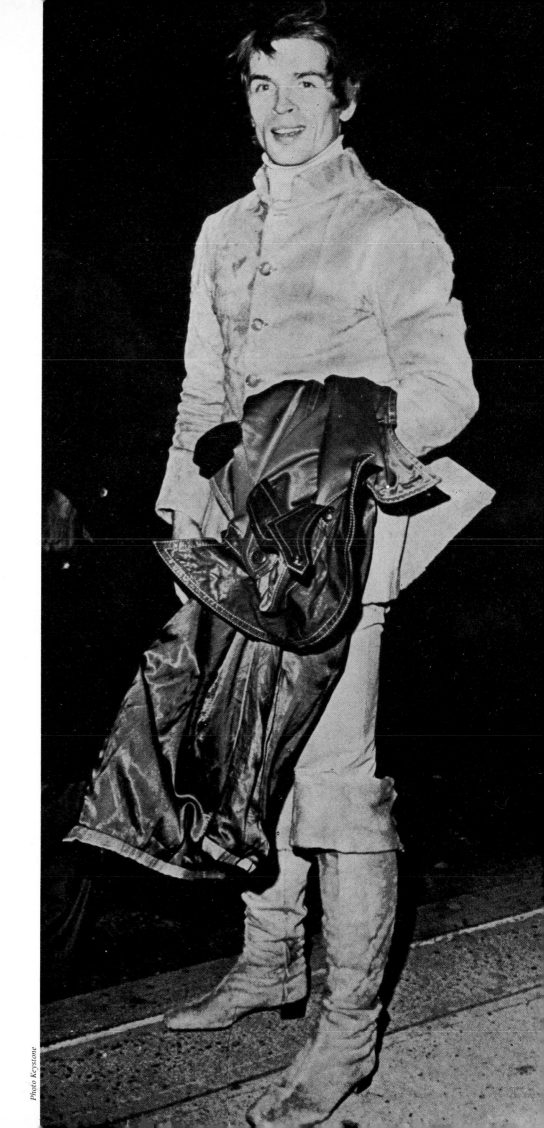

Arriving for the première of his *Don Quixote* film in New York

Photo Camera Press

After a rehearsal in the Acropolis
Theatre in Athens, Nureyev talks to
Margot Fonteyn, King Constantine,
Queen Anne-Marie, Princess Irene,
Prince Michael and Sir Frederick
Ashton

Photo Vartoogian

Counting the number of times he had
scored off Dick Cavett during a
television interview in America

from company to company, from big stages to small ones, from one production to another and working with a list of different ballerinas long enough to form a complete corps de ballet at the Bolshoi. Never, surely, has one dancer danced so much with so many.

The adventures of his early life inevitably changed into professional projects and achievements, and though his contests with managements have continued, his battles have mainly been artistic ones. From time to time non-ballet events interrupted the dance narrative, often minor events blown up through the publicity power of his larger-than-life personality. On his first visit to Canada, with the Royal Ballet, he was briefly hauled into a police-station for walking across the street against

Dancing with Elizabeth Taylor at the Dorchester Hotel, London

Photo Syndication International

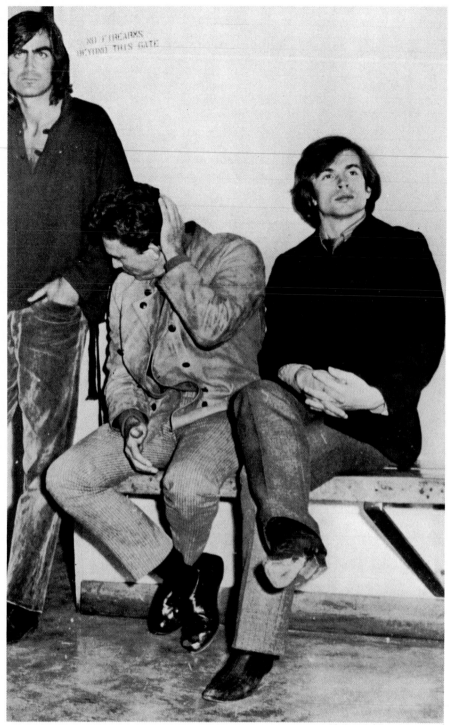

In a San Francisco police station after being arrested with Fonteyn at a party where they had been suspected of taking drugs

Photo United Press International

the traffic-lights; he was knocked over by a motor-scooter in the King's Road in London; he was rehearsing with Fonteyn in Bath when the news came that her husband had been seriously wounded in an assassination attempt in Panama; he was pushed into a Monte Carlo swimming pool by a photographer (the photographer followed, camera and all) and shoved a member of the Milan corps de ballet who stood in his way on stage (she threatened to sue); he had his tonsils out in London and was arrested in San Francisco, together with Fonteyn, after the police had received the improbable tip-off that they might be caught taking drugs at a party. He told an outraged conductor in Vienna who was succeeding in making a waltz in *Swan Lake* sound like Johann

Photo Snowdon

All the fun of a Vienna fair

Sailing off the coast of Israel

Photo Joe Bangay

Photo Zoë Dominic

A wig serves as a try-out for a beard

Photo Snowdon

Applying the strong make-up needed
for an opera-house performance

Strauss to 'go back to his glockenspiel', and threw a shrimp pâté at a celebrated critic at a dinner party in Australia. These were the kind of stories which the popular press loved to hear. The exciting image of a 'Rimbaud of the Steppes' (as Ashton once called him, with more imagination than accuracy) was slowly built up by a process in which an ounce of truth was added to a pound of gossip and news-page invention. He was of course several times reported to be engaged to be married.

But the real events in his career were of a different order. They consisted of his first film appearance (performing in *Les Sylphides* and *Le Corsaire* in *An Evening with the Royal Ballet* in December 1962); his first specially created role (with Fonteyn in Ashton's *Marguerite and Armand* in March 1963); his own first production (the last act of *La Bayadère* for the Royal Ballet in November 1963); his first reconstruction of a nineteenth-century three-act classic (*Raymonda* for the Royal Ballet

Designer Nicholas Georgiadis tries out a new costume

Photo Snowdon

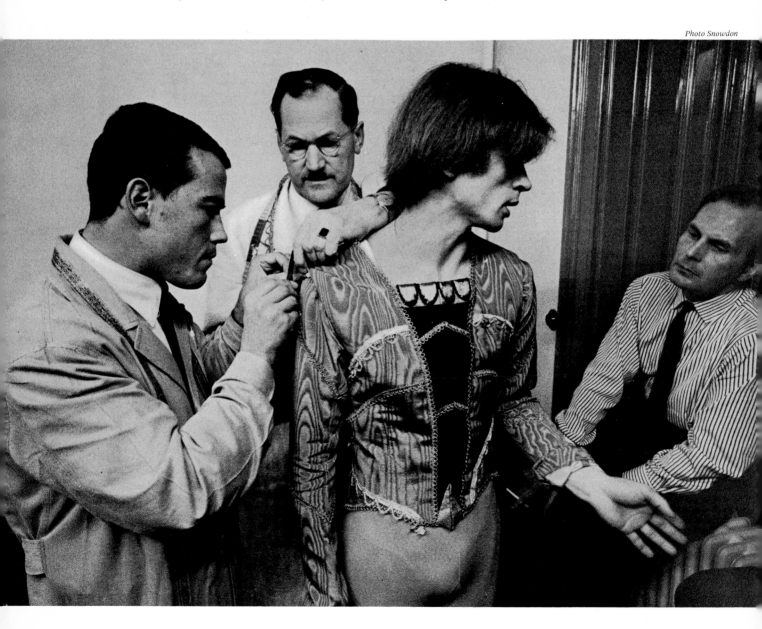

Photo Zoë Dominic

Hunter and prey: Cecil Beaton stalks
Nureyev during a photo-call

touring company at Spoleto in June 1964); his first personal ballet
(*Tancredi* to a score by Hans Werner Henze in Vienna in May 1966); his
first performance in a modern-dance ballet to electronic music (in van
Dantzig's *Monument for a Dead Boy* with the Dutch National Ballet in
December 1968); his debut as a film-director (directing – with aid from
Robert Helpmann – his own production of *Don Quixote* in which he
danced the leading role with the Australian Ballet, shot in Melbourne in
November 1972); his first season with a group of his own (dancing in all
four ballets in programmes at the Palais des Sports in Paris in June
1974); his first disc (as the Soldier in Stravinsky's *The Soldier's Tale*,
with Glenda Jackson and Michèal MacLiammòir, recorded in London in
August 1975); and his first appearance as a film actor, as the hero of Ken
Russell's *Rudolph Valentino*, shot in August 1976.

This pattern of activities – sandwiched between a gruelling schedule

39

Photo Keystone

On holiday

of travelling, rehearsals and performances (in the summer and autumn of 1964 he contrived to mount two full-length ballets, *Raymonda* and *Swan Lake*, within three months) – reveals not only an incredibly sustained level of achievement but a steadily expanding range. The world of ballet has always tended to be a claustrophobic hothouse, a private shrine with its own gods and worshippers, a specialist field from which the general public has been largely excluded. The width and range of Nureyev's activities have meant that he has become an international star whose name strikes echoes in fields far outside the ballet. His personality has burst out of the plush-lined corridors of the opera house; he has pushed dance into unprecedented realms of popular recognition.

The second act in a play is traditionally devoted to the development of the plot. In the drama of Nureyev's career the character of the hero has filled out in its middle period in a way which few people could have foreseen, and the story has acquired such a rich variety that the style, and even the locations, of future instalments are hard to guess. It seems certain that there will be some surprising twists; the pace of the narrative shows no signs of slackening.

Photo Hans Hammarsgiold

Curtain-call with Fonteyn

The Man

For all artists the axiom that 'the style is the man' is at least partly true; but one of the aims of classical dance training is to impose an impersonal uniform discipline, and many good dancers become little more than anonymous illustrations of academic virtues. Nureyev has never been that kind of dancer. His approach is invariably human, warm-blooded and personal. His qualities as a dancer are inseparably connected with his character. Every facet of his temperament is relevant to an understanding of his work and art.

The most immediately noticeable characteristic is an exceptional singleness of aim, coupled with a range of natural gifts which seems specially designed to achieve it. Drive and flexibility (two hallmarks of his dancing) are perhaps his greatest assets, but they form only part of his armoury. He seemed to arrive in the West fully equipped for a conflict which he has waged unremittingly ever since – a struggle not only with competitors but to win some private battle within himself. He came out fighting and he has never relaxed. He allows no distractions from a performance, neither illness nor fatigue nor disagreements nor personal considerations. With ferocity and cunning and charm he has pressed forward, sparing neither others nor himself.

The publicity which followed his arrival in the West propelled him into the headlines like a rocket. Wise heads were shaken and predictions put about that he would flare briefly and drop into oblivion. His dancing encouraged these forecasts. Each appearance worked on the audience like a minor explosion: his fire and abandon, combined with an appearance of waif-like vulnerability, seemed too precarious to last.

The impulsive streak in his personality and the dionysiac style of his performances were seized on by the press to create for him an exciting, if rather inaccurate, public image. His late hours (normal, in fact, for theatre people) and his habitual look of a long-haired urchin – it was months before he replaced his favourite pair of bedraggled trousers and worn-out shoes – were ripe material for the gossip columns, which manufactured a character designed to contrast romantically with our own well-disciplined dancers.

There was a grain of truth in the exaggerated picture. Nonconformity was at the root of Nureyev's rebellion, and resistance to authority was

42

Photo Mike Davis

his guideline. If his dancing broke the conventions of classical propriety, his private temperament was equally unorthodox. He haunted night clubs and restaurants and made an international variety of acquaintances. He devoured the plays and films and pictures he had read about but never seen. He spent his new money freely on books and records, on a fast car and a house in the mountains in the South of France and became a prime ingredient in the 'swinging London' of the sixties. If he was often lonely and unhappy he did not let on. A glint of schoolboy defiance smouldered in the news-page snaps and in the corner of his eye while he took his curtain calls, with a gesture of half-ironic arrogance (he never deigned to accept flowers in public). He avoided formal occasions, ignored letters and invitations and skipped in and out of the capitals of the West as though he were invisible. He got to know the full range of attractions of a Western metropolis without ever quite losing his way in them. A kind of child-like candour protected him even in his most extravagant escapades: 'The trouble is, I suppose I do not have the courage to be as wicked as I want,' he confessed mischievously to Fonteyn.

What was disconcerting was his headlong involvement in whatever lay at hand, whether work or play. The least vague of characters (and the least tolerant of woolly thinking or indecisive action in others), he would, and still will, pour an alarming concentration of energy into successions of seemingly unrelated activities. The same spotlight of attention is turned in quick succession on to the movement of a dancer's eyes, the exact significance of an adjective or the timbre of an instrument in the orchestra. He combines a piercing eye for detail with a sharp brain and quick reactions. He is at once shrewd, tough, easily hurt and cynical. The acute sensibilities of a forest pygmy seem preserved in a member of the jet set.

This curious sense of being simultaneously more primitive and more sophisticated than others runs right through his deeply contradictory character, and emerges clearly in his dancing. Most modern Russians are profoundly influenced by nineteenth-century values, both moral and aesthetic. Nureyev – perhaps protected by being so passionately an outsider – never revealed the smallest symptom of this kind of national provincialism. He seemed not so much to reject conventional taste and opinions as never to have entertained them. In Paris, London and New York, in art and music, in social style and sense of humour, in theatrical awareness and personal manner, he appeared not only at home but discriminating. He seemed from the very first perfectly at ease with a complicated contract or an airline timetable; he seemed to know by instinct how to handle a camera and to adjust a ballet production for television techniques. The only thing which frightens him – badly – is flying, but he spends half his life in the air.

This is not to say that he has adopted a West European personality. He retains a strong suggestion of ancient Russia, with its cruelty and generosity, sensuality and hardiness. Both by choice and through necessity he leads the life of a nomad. Like his Tartar forebears he puts

Photo Arthur Todd

Photo Leslie E Spatt

down no roots, but lives off his environment and then, suddenly, moves on. Unsentimental and unnostalgic, there is little room in his life for the non-functional. His books and records and films and tapes are material for future work; the gifts he receives from admirers are enjoyed like toys; even the massively sumptuous style he fitfully adopts for his own background seems designed as a practical decor for living.

When he moves he travels light, planning his departure at the last possible moment and abruptly announcing his arrival. Like most habitual travellers he sticks to well-worn clothes, familiar surroundings and old friends. He fills – personally, with practical meticulousness – a battered grip or two, which may remain only half unpacked after a stay

Photo Cecil Beaton

Photo Peter Friedrich

Photo Roy Round

of weeks. He camps out in the most luxurious hotel room as if it were a tent, or a corner or one of the portable palaces of the old Russian empresses. He has no 'home'; but his house perched in the hills above Monte Carlo is his favourite retreat and London has been his base; he maintains there a house of dishevelled grandeur in which he entertains with regal informality. Unlike most theatrical characters he prefers playing host to guest.

The constant change of scene fits his temperament. His rapid reactions, his instant discharges of energy and his quick capacities all spring from an exceptionally fast metabolism, both mental and physical. He recklessly gives out dynamics during rehearsals or a performance but afterwards he may suddenly flake out with fatigue. In the middle of a sentence his voice will fade and his attention wander: his eyes glaze and he seems barely conscious, with hardly the strength to drag himself to a chair. But after a few hours broken sleep (he is a confirmed insomniac) a blistering bath and, if possible – best of all – a massage, he will be back in circulation, as outgoing and ruthlessly demanding as ever.

The capacity to consume fuel like an aero-engine, to transform his intake into energy at a superhuman speed, results in an abnormally quick consumption rate, both mental and physical. He does not like sustained concentration on a single subject; his method of thinking is lateral and spasmodic. He will reflect on a problem over a long period, but it will be in short snatches. He likes to discuss business affairs in the dressing room between the acts rather than in a secluded private office.

Photo A & M Ziverts

Photo Henri Cartier-Bresson

way into the ballet and to fight his way up once he was inside it. He neither sought nor received help. He operates on the principle that nobody is going to watch over his interests better than himself. The result is a disarming realism and a disconcerting resourcefulness.

The bewildering complexity of his schedule is matched by a Protean complication of character. No two people have the same opinion of Nureyev because he rarely presents the same personality twice. He can move – at a speed which catches even himself off-guard – from icy disdain to a self-deprecating grin, from warmth and courtesy to cutting sarcasm or an outburst of rage and rudeness (almost invariably about work). He can be witty and talkative one moment, silent and withdrawn the next. He is still partly the mischievous urchin from Bashkir; but the other parts are a dangerous mixture in which suspicion and sensitivity, aggression and ambition, egotism and a ruthlessness directed equally at himself and others battle against a nature which is basically gentle, generous, somewhat shy and – justifiably – lacking in a sense of security.

He can be outrageously egocentric and demanding, yet accepts setbacks and compromises with total realism. He likes the amenities offered by the rich but his own interest in money is spasmodic and superficial: it is a by-product, not a spur, and he will readily dance for a low fee for a friend or a company he admires. He totally lacks the instincts of the snob or career-socialite, never bothering to keep up influential acquaintanceship. He can be unfair, unreasonable, exasperatingly capricious, crude and rude. He is basically untrusting and often prejudiced. He can sulk and grumble and he has a strong streak of Russian secretiveness and an appetite for plotting. But (this is what makes him a good subject for the interviewer), he is alarmingly candid; he may keep quiet but he does not lie – and in any case his theatrical features betray every thought. He seldom refuses time and attention (or practical assistance) to any dancer asking for advice or help; but to the lazy or casual or unserious he can be brutally unsympathetic.

The changes which have marked his character since he arrived in the West have arisen less from exposure to new stimuli than from the simple process of growing older. When he arrived he was a boy, now he is a man, but the follow-through is direct. The working dinner may have replaced the night club, but his demeanour contrives to blur the difference; tea has taken the place of whisky and vodka, but he has not lost his taste for adventures, risk and instant changes of plan.

Nureyev's great asset, both as an artist and as a human being, is that the star has never swallowed up the man. He is theatrical to the backbone, expanding in front of an audience with an instinct for dramatic effect; but he is not a poseur. He can be arrogant (though people meeting him for the first time are often surprised at his modesty – they take the hauteur of his stage princes for the real thing), but he is not vain: he has no taste for daintiness or fanciful decorations; he never wears personal jewellery; there is scarcely a mirror in his house and there is usually a hole in his sock. He is a realistic critic of his own work,

With Margot Fonteyn

Photo Frederika Davis

Photo Jack Mitchell

and touchingly pleased when he feels he has brought off a good performance. Insatiably inquisitive, he prefers asking questions to giving answers.

Nureyev is an assemblage of contradictory qualities in which each element preserves its identity in an extreme form. They are held together by an outsize ego and animated by colossal drive. The tensions remain, and can lead — especially when he is nervous about a performance — to prickliness and explosions. But in the end every ingredient serves his chosen career. The charm and talent, the physical toughness and intellectual dexterity, the adaptability and endurance, the dominating presence, flexible temperament, nonconformism, independence, the mixture of courage and caution, the nerve, energy and unremitting self interest all contribute to a character in which form and function are virtually identical.

With Erik Bruhn

With Yvette Chauviré

The Dancer

Photo Jack Mitchell

Preparation for pirouette, with Erik
Bruhn

Dance begins with the dancer; his body is his voice, his brush, his pen. Its conformation, capabilities and limitations are the quintessence of his achievements. Nureyev's line, height, weight and proportions, and the consistency of his muscles, are the *matière* which his artistry directs. They are the battleground on which he has had to win his first victories. They are relevant at all times, though many kinds of skill and artifice may be added to them; they are not to be disguised or evaded, but used.

Nureyev is of medium height. He has a small head, a rather long strong neck, and wide shoulders tapering dramatically to an exceptionally small waist. His arms were thin when he was young, but work has filled them out; they are slightly double-jointed at the elbow, giving them the disposition to curve in the same way as his extra-supple fingers. He is not elegantly long in the leg; his thighs and calves are strongly muscled, and his feet are small and wide – their pliability led, in mid-career, to strains and difficulties. His back and shoulders are powerfully modelled.

His features are not classical and regular but theatrically expressive. Large, well-spaced eyes under fiercely arching eyebrows combine with a short, slightly tilted nose with flaring nostrils to give an impression of intensity which is offset by a full and sensuous mouth. Dramatically high cheekbones give a triangular effect to a face which is actually built round strong, square jaws. His hair is very fine and light, with a reddish tint (in childhood it was much more blond). His expression is disconcertingly mobile; the soulful big-lidded eyes narrow suddenly into slits of suspicion, anger or amusement, the mouth changes from a sulky pout to a wide, many-crinkled grin. It is a good face for the stage, with well defined features which fall naturally into expressiveness. His danger has always, in fact, been that of being over-explicit: he has only to open his mouth to breathe and he registers passion or despair. The striking, instantly recognizable features have a kind of wild beauty which has made them into a romantic pin-up in many a lonely bedroom and a favourite subject for (invariably unposed) portraits.

The contradictions in his face match not only his temperament but his physique, in which a heroic build is offset by a supple grace which has often been compared to that of a cat; it would have to be of the jungle kind, for the sinuous sensuality is never without a hint of

Photo Snowdon

Photo Costa

menace. When he first arrived he suggested a young panther; now he
seems nearer to a full-grown lion.

With Vera Volkova in Copenhagen

Though it is laced with oriental softness, Nureyev's dancing is
entirely positive and masculine: he has not Nijinsky's androgynous
ambiguity. But the effect he makes can be double-edged, with a sexual
magnetism which seems to transcend gender and is discernible by both
men and women. He never excels as an asexual sprite or symbol, but
he has few rivals as a stage lover. This quality is backed by a presence of
almost hypnotic force (he has always wanted to play Rasputin). He has
sometimes been accused of 'hogging' a performance when in fact he has
spent much of the time merely sitting or standing.

The benefits conferred by this inborn attribute have had their
disadvantages: every detail in an evening's dancing comes under
special scrutiny, the smallest slip seems monumental. He has never been
free from criticism (less from dancers than from critics); something of
his fighting attitude to life seeps through his work, and he has battled

Photo Jack Mitchell

his way to pre-eminence against swirling and often opposing currents of professional discussion. Often some innovation (such as the series of *entrechats* in *Giselle* Act II or the solo at the end of *Swan Lake* Act I) which rouses urgent protest when he introduces it becomes traditional a few years later. In the same way his excursions into the modern style, which were deplored when he first embarked on them, have led the way for other classically-trained dancers. He is a balletic ice-breaker, fortunately equipped with a sturdy engine and a psychological armour tough enough to withstand the pressures.

His pioneering experiments start paradoxically from a fanatical feeling for tradition. He was trained in the strictest classical conventions, and he adheres to strictly classical principles. He is fiercely disciplined about work. He takes at the most two weeks holiday in a year, and daily practice is an essential part of his routine (Sundays often include filming, television or rehearsals). Nothing is allowed to deflect him from his regular, methodical training. It is a ritual as important to his mind as to his body. For modern work he may do Graham-style exercises, but normally he goes through the conventional classical ballet syllabus. He has had few equals in the traditional style. Sir Frederick Ashton describes him as 'a great classical dancer', and Dame Ninette de Valois has remarked sadly: 'I think he should concentrate on what he does better than anyone else, dancing the classics perfectly.' Yet he has scored notable successes in modern barefoot roles: some critics have even preferred him in them.

His approach to non-classical dance was a mixture of hope and caution. He is well aware of the strains imposed on muscles trained for different stresses; to relax is, for a classically taught dancer, often as difficult as it is for a modern dancer to tighten up. His first experiment with the novel idiom was in *Ropes of Time*, created for him and the Royal Ballet by Rudi van Dantzig in 1970. The experience proved so satisfying that he appeared in the next two years both with the Paul Taylor company in America and with Maurice Béjart in Brussels. The mixture of weight and plasticity – both important in modern dance – which he brought to these roles was stretched even further in Glen Tetley ballets at Covent Garden and, later, at the Paris Opéra. Finally, his adoption of the modern idiom was celebrated when Martha Graham, the founder and arch-priestess of the movement, in 1975 created specially for him the ballet *Lucifer*, quickly followed by *The Scarlet Letter*. He had provided the missing link between the two styles – a role which may have far-reaching consequences.

His range covers not only different styles but different types of role within them. The proudest of princes, he makes also the most mischievous of barbers (in *Don Quixote*) or a broad comedy clown. He is the quintessential romantic lover (in *Romeo and Juliet* or *Marguerite and Armand*) but revels in the aged antics of Dr Drosselmeyer (in *The Nutcracker*) the cool lyricism of *Aureole*, the pathos of *The Prodigal Son* or the passion of *Lucifer* or *Le Sacre du Printemps*. He loves to switch in one evening from mood to mood – though he is professionally careful

Photo Snowdon

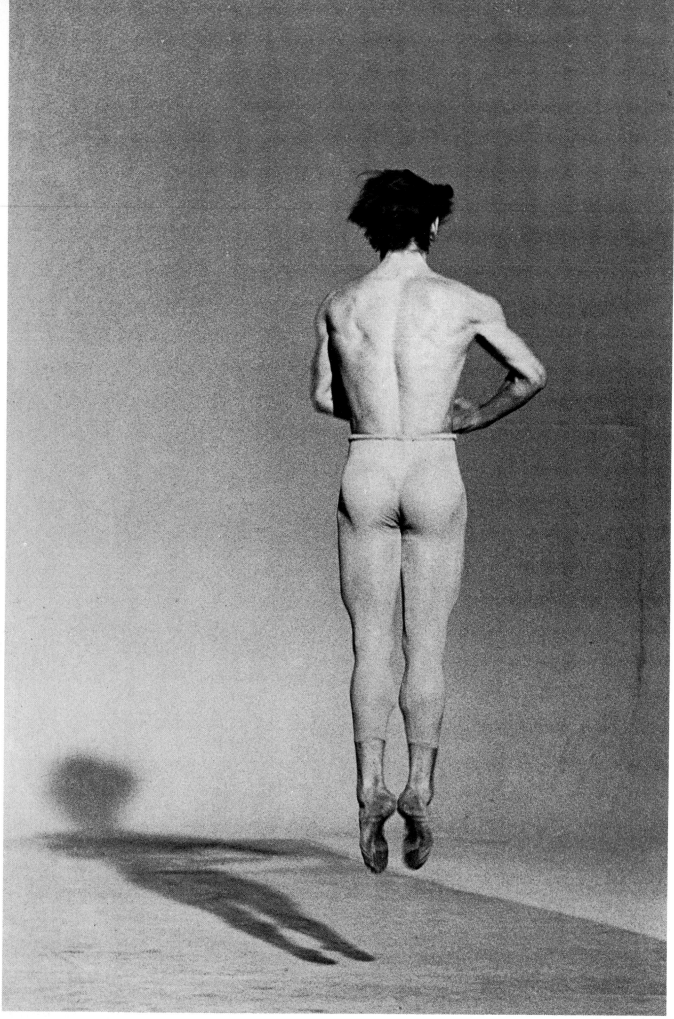

Photo Giancarlo Botti

Photo Rosemary Winckley

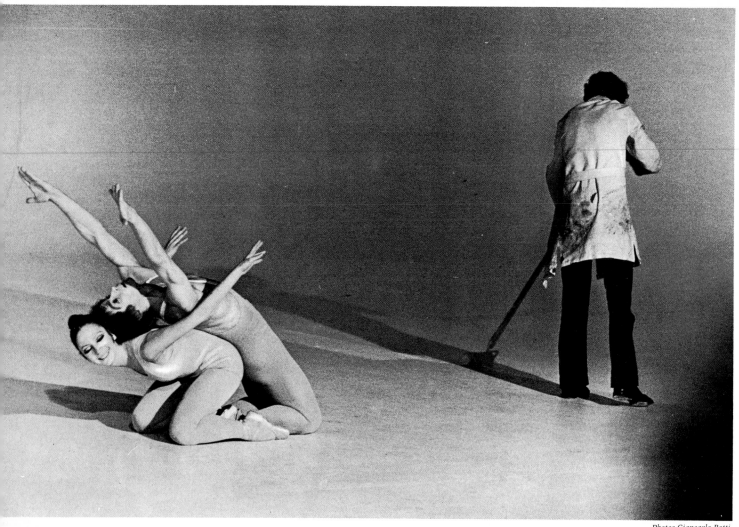

Photos Giancarlo Botti

about the order. Muscles carefully loosened for a modern role cannot be quickly tightened up for classical virtuosities.

His technical knowledge is profound. When he arrived in the West it was his fire and abandon which first struck his audiences; but his fellow-dancers soon discovered that they were based on a sharply analytical mind and an almost pernickety attention to detail. Fonteyn has described how in their first days together, he cured her long-standing difficulty with *fouettés* by a single practical hint, and he has since proved a much valued technical coach to many dancers; as a partner he is demanding – he knows what he wants and is obstinate about getting it – and insists on the need for close artistic (not necessarily personal) sympathy; but few men have more skill in presenting ballerinas to advantage, nor more varied experience in their different problems. If he knows they are giving their utmost he is infinitely patient; if he feels they are not, he is not interested.

Aware that the career of a dancer – particularly of a male dancer, who has the additional strain of lifting and supporting his partner – is pitiably short, and intent on extracting more and more from the capacities he has been granted, Nureyev is gluttonous for new roles. He will never miss a chance of a full-length classical ballet – no dancer dances more of these in a year – but apart from that he aims at adding continually to his repertoire. He will often take on an awkward date

with a relatively undistinguished company purely to acquire a new role. He searches continually for a choreographer who will add one more dimension to his already Protean dancing personality.

This impression of daemonic energy marked his style from the start. The natural 'voice' of Russian dancers is pitched lower than that of their counterparts in the West, and Nureyev – though his range is wide – is constitutionally the equivalent of a baritone, not a tenor. As the old Tchaikovsky classics were written for Russian 'voices', he has the advantage which most of his compatriots enjoy in them, as compared with the lighter, more lyrical dancer typical of the West. He has an instinctive sense of line, adjusting an arm or the angle of his head subconsciously to maintain the flow of movement from end to end of his body, but he is not built for delicate long-limbed elegance. He is (as Nijinsky clearly was) a sculptural rather than a linear dancer, exploiting the contrast between his narrow, flexible waist and his powerful shoulders and back. He is very aware of the spaces enclosed by his limbs and by the interaction between himself and his partner. His arm movements are always full and generous and his legs mark out the stage patterns with emphasis. When he moves fast it is with the speed of a projectile, not a dart. He never loses the quality which sculptors call 'mass' – a kind of concentrated volume and density which lends presence to a movement.

This characteristic emerges clearly in the big leaps which were the most obvious striking feature of his first appearances. He does not shoot up quickly and lightly from the ground as though gravity did not exist; he does not skim or fly, drift or flicker. When he jumps there is a perceptible build-up of power, a tremendous thrust, and then a great lift-off: once in the air he soars and sails rather than floats. It is the leap of a big salmon, rather than the spring of a deer. Karsavina described it as 'space-devouring'.

He has an instinctive panache – he is a master at swirling a cloak or flourishing a hat – and the capacity to dance slowly, the most difficult of all technical feats, requiring the strength and control to sustain a *legato* through acrobatic contortions. But he can move fast when he wants to. He will change into 'overdrive' and assume an astonishing velocity in the final *manège* of a long solo. His beats are clear and strong, his

Rehearsing Marguerite and Armand, with Fonteyn

Photo Zoë Dominic

Photo Zoë Dominic

pirouettes are done with a force which sometimes pushes them off balance: they are not just decorative spins but an expression of dynamics as forceful as a jump. He rarely 'cheats' in his *tours en l'air* but insists on a correct take-off and a landing in proper fifth position. He combines integrity of feeling with integrity of technique.

Rehearsing *Marguerite and Armand*, with Fonteyn

The all-out attack which Nureyev will launch on a movement has its built-in handicaps; he has never been an even performer. But accidents or misfires do not disconcert him as they might a less buoyant character. At the première of his own first production at Covent Garden, *La Bayadère*, he danced himself clean into the wings, but reappeared nonchalantly a few moments later; when one shoe flew off during a glittering gala at the Coliseum, he instantly removed the other and finished the solo barefoot, to increased applause. His smallest reactions are theatrical. This inbuilt uncertainty (an American writer has aptly described it as 'dancing without a net') has helped to lend Nureyev's performances an excitement missing from technically more assured

Rehearsing *Romeo and Juliet*,
with Fonteyn

Rehearsal with Fonteyn

Photo Snowdon

occasions. His temperamental addiction to risk communicates to the audience a sense of danger. 'What do you think I do every night?' replied Nureyev, when asked if he were a gambler.

After many years' successive appearances, this impact has inevitably lost its first shock effect. Some artists – like Nijinsky – acquired a mystique through rarity: others, such as Pavlova, made their reputation through the widest contact with the public. Through his international roster of stage performances, his television appearances and the world-wide distribution of his films, Nureyev's work is familiar to millions. That his reputation has withstood this sustained and wide-angled floodlight is remarkable.

It is not, however, fortuitous. Though he is a master improviser, programming his life from minute to minute, he moves within a long-term strategy. When accepting future engagements – sometimes two years in advance – he makes sure that they include a regular ration of the classics. ('It is like going to the doctor,' he explains) and in a single programme he likes to insist on a 'meaty' number as well as some restrained and subtle interpretation. In the same way he has carefully added to his roles to suit his age, gradually fortifying virtuoso acrobatics with strong dramatic parts and modern ballets demanding a different kind of technique; and his essays into speaking and purely acting roles have been made at a time when they can carry his career forward into maturity. A shrewd, indeed cunning intelligence lies behind the impulsiveness.

Nureyev is an intensely personal dancer even in the classics. He has never been just an exceptional exponent of the academic norm. He declares that it took him at least five years on stage to develop his own style – it is part Kirov, part Royal Ballet and other influences ('I arrived with the baggage but I learned in the West what to do with it,' he explains) – and he accepts and indeed welcomes individuality in others. When asked if an interpretation by a dancer is right, he often answers: 'It is right for him.' What he has searched for is a way of dancing which fully and truthfully reflects himself. The explosive energy and attack; the plasticity which exploits every inch of his body (he has the Russian gift of an expressive back); the lightning changes from direct positive drive to capriciousness – they all spring from his tough but elusive personality. The panache, the haunted romanticism, the defiant walk round the stage before a variation like a champion staking out his territory, the rippling runs as smooth as cream, the sudden *pas de chat* like a hawk pouncing on its prey, the mischievous schoolboy swagger, the slow, soft arching leap and the dramatically gentle finish – these idiosyncrasies work for him because they are part of his nature. His secret is not the acquisition of a set of tricks or techniques, but the gradual unveiling of his whole personality. He has a giant ego and he has harnessed all of it to his dancing.

He knows his own body perfectly, but as an instrument not as an object of affection. He is totally unnarcissistic – a quality rare in stage performers, and one which gives conviction to his romantic partner-

With Sir Frederick Ashton

ships. He demands a similar outgoing response from the ballerina: 'she never looks at me, only the audience,' is his most damning complaint. At all times and in all parts he exudes a positive and powerful humanity. This can be a difficulty: his Oberon and his Death (in *Song of the Earth*) are not spirits but mortals in disguise. But in compensation the vitality and reality which he pours into his princes and romantic lovers, his young tearaways and old dotards works on his partners like a shot of adrenalin and animates the whole stage.

Nureyev's commitment to dancing is total. It is, as he has expressed it, his only 'avenue of fulfilment'. For its sake he has fought and sweated, suffered, quarrelled, insulted and borne insults, schemed, dreamed and made bitter sacrifices. It takes priority in his life over everything and everybody; his loyalty to it is unquestioning. It is both the means of his living and the end. It is not a gesture for the benefit for others but an instinctive egoistic existential act. He can say, paraphrasing Descartes, *'Je danse donc je suis'* – 'I dance, therefore I am.'

With Ninette de Valois

Photo Snowdon

With Lubov Tchernicheva

Photo Reg Wilson

Photo Keith Money

Encouraged by this venture, he tackled the following year two of the most massive productions in the classical repertoire. *Raymonda* was the last of Petipa's big successes, dating from 1898, and, though popular in Russia, had never been welcomed in the West in the same way as the Tchaikovsky classics: it lacks the yearning romanticism of *Swan Lake* and the glitter of *The Sleeping Beauty*.

Nureyev was commissioned to mount it on the Royal Ballet's touring company for the Spoleto Festival. The designer, Beni Montresor, decided at the last moment to adopt a modified modernism; the company's talents proved hardly equal to the difficult dancing; and a personal crisis (her husband's dangerous relapse) removed Margot Fonteyn from the vital ballerina role between the dress rehearsal and the première. Doreen Wells stepped in gallantly, but the production showed more promise than achievement. Nothing daunted, Nureyev mounted it in a much revised version for the Australian Ballet the following year, for the Zurich Opera Ballet in 1972 and for American Ballet Theatre in New York in 1975.

These last two, virtually identical, productions were designed by the artist he had always had in mind, Nicholas Georgiadis, and contained many new ideas and much new choreography. From the first Nureyev

Nicholas Georgiadis' model for Abderachman's tent in *Raymonda*, Act II

Swan Lake, Act I: Nureyev's solo in the setting by Nicholas Georgiadis

92

had contributed a great deal, though the Petipa highlights were reproduced intact. He is always ready, in fact anxious, to alter and improve on first attempts; the changes are usually towards a more convincing motivation for the action and more variety in the dancing. He overlaid the straightforward narrative of *Raymonda* with the suggestion that the heroine's abduction by a glamorous Saracen was a dream projection of her virginal anxieties about her approaching marriage, and he injected a number of new 'character' numbers, a *pas de deux* and solos for the usually rather colourless hero. He is much attracted by Indian and Persian art and something of their convoluted style has crept into his own very personal contributions: some of these, though – for instance a striking *pas de trois* in the last act – have been widely mistaken for original Petipa. Sumptuous, full-blooded and positive, this is a production which reflects the curious streak of baroque splendour which underlay late-ninteenth-century taste.

Within a few months Nureyev – who had danced all performances of the hero in his own production – was in Vienna tackling another formidable task, *Swan Lake*. This was a ballet in which he had danced many times in Russia and on which he had strong views. He was not satisfied with the normal ending – which he felt untrue to the tragic undertones of the music – and he wanted to build up the role of the hero to make a proper counterpart to the ballerina. He accordingly made his Prince set a dark mood from the very beginning (he had the same aim in the solo he choreographed for the Royal Ballet version in 1962), gave him an extra dance in Act I, with his friends, and adopted a variation on the ending used by Bourmeister in Moscow, with the Prince drowned in the overflowing lake. Whether from the evocative performances of Fonteyn and himself or from the production, the ballet struck a note of romanticism deeper than in the Sergeyev version traditional in the West. (It is not conveyed by the filmed translation.) The only moderately expert Viennese company acquired a temporary stylishness and finish.

To tackle two such major productions at the very start of his career was certainly courageous; he now felt ready to try his hand at an original work. In May 1966 he flew to Vienna and shortly afterwards he emerged as the hero of his own first ballet, *Tancredi*. The score, by Hans Werner Henze, had been adapted from an earlier ballet and given a new scenario; in Nureyev's version it had a heavily psychological plot, based on the theme of the many strands in a personality. It was a viable subject and it led to some striking dance passages – especially a scene in which Nureyev seemed to split into several *alter egos* – and a beautiful skeletal set by Barry Kay. But it did not add up to a successful whole and it was dropped from the repertoire after two years.

His next production showed not only greater experience, but more confidence. The subject was completely sympathetic to him. *The Sleeping Beauty* has always been regarded as the hallmark of the Maryinsky company; it had been preserved with loving integrity by the Kirov, and Nureyev knew it well. But he had no thought of simply reproducing the Leningrad production. He dreamed of a version which would truly reflect the grandeur of Louis XIV's Versailles, not stage glamour but the genuine pomp and majesty of the seventeenth-century France court, peopled by real characters. The huge stage of La Scala, Milan, was ideal for such a spectacle and Nicholas Georgiadis the ideal designer to fill it out. The result was as imposing as Diaghilev's legendary Bakst production must have been – grandiose, resonant, solemn. All traces of pantomime charm were removed; even the witch Carabosse became a sophisticated dowager in a court creaking with outworn imperial heritages; only Aurora and the Prince, fresh and young, suggested a new world. In the last scene nothing has changed after a hundred years, except their love – a small potent seed holding the future. Nureyev has modified some details for other companies since, mainly to suit less lavishly equipped theatres. With its realism, sense of history and weighty style, it remains the most typical of all his productions, a richly sculptured vision in which the dancing is half Petipa, half Nureyev.

Barry Kay's setting for *Tancredi*: Nureyev with the *corps de ballet*

Photo Fayer

95

Photo Zoë Dominic

Photo Shuhei Iwamoto

Don Quixote (Robert Helpmann) duels
with Gamache (Colin Peasley) in *Don
Quixote*, designed by Barry Kay

Above left
The Garland Dance in Act I of *The
Sleeping Beauty*, designed by Nicholas
Georgiadis
Left
King Florestan (Donald Barclay) dances
a *sarabande* with his Queen (Linda
Darrell) in Act III of *The Sleeping Beauty*.
Costumes by Nicholas Georgiadis

In that same year, 1966, he mounted another full-length work, of a completely contrasting character – *Don Quixote*. This light-hearted entertainment had been one of Petipa's first successes, in 1869. Nureyev's production for the Vienna Opera, in which he danced the mischievous young barber, showed a side of his character which had not yet been revealed elsewhere – a puckish sense of fun. Building on the version he had known in Russia, he invented much new 'business' (for example a comic duel between the tottery old Knight and the foppish Gamache) and many new numbers. He also – gradually developing his line of thought as he mounted successive productions for the Australian and Marseilles companies – changed the order of the dances and added an important new section, a romantic *pas de deux* beneath the old windmill, to music (borrowed from *La Bayadère*) by the

Photo Michelangelo Durazzo

same composer, Minkus. All zest and sparkle, this production had a pace and panache abetted by Barry Kay's designs.

The handling of the crowd scenes and the corps de ballet showed how much he had learnt, and this was confirmed in his next big production, *The Nutcracker* for the Royal Swedish Ballet in November 1967, revised the following year for the Royal Ballet. This was a drastic transformation. The ballet, originally mounted in St Petersburg in 1892, had been planned by Petipa but choreographed by Ivanov – not very successfully, it seems, as the original dances have practically all disappeared, apart from a heavily amended *pas de deux*. It had, however, established itself as an international favourite, with an innocent charm which made it suitable for Christmas outings – a tinselly entertainment to be viewed indulgently.

Nureyev changed the whole tone by taking the subject, and more specially the score – which contains some of Tchaikovsky's finest theatre music – seriously. Aiming, as always, at a logical structure which would unify a hitherto piecemeal plot, he wove a psychological twist into the story. It became the dream of the child-heroine who was also the ballerina – a half-nightmare stemming from family tensions. Instead of being scaled down into an adult's view of nursery fun, the vision was blown up as though in a child's imagination – a device which

The footlights make a temporary seat while Nureyev takes a dress rehearsal

La Bayadère

The big roles for a male classical dancer in the West used to be very few – the Prince in *Swan Lake* and *The Sleeping Beauty*, the Duke in *Giselle* and (if he worked in New York or London) the principal in *The Nutcracker* or one or two modern three-acters. In Russia several full-length nineteenth-century classics have survived, offering important dancing roles to the hero. One of these is *La Bayadère*, produced by Petipa in St Petersburg in 1877.

It is a long, rambling ballet in the oriental style; the scene is set in India, the heroine is a temple dancer and there are numbers for priests, concubines, fakirs, and acrobats. The heroine is murdered by her jealous rival (who hides a snake in a basket of flowers); the hero is thrown into prison and there, lulled by the hashish smoke from a fellow captive's pipe, he dreams of his dead beloved. She appears, with a bevy of companions, from the Kingdom of the Shades and dances before him.

In the original production this was followed by a finale on conventional lines, but this was dropped some time ago; Act IV became almost a short ballet on its own – a languorous scene in which Petipa miraculously translated geometry into romantic poetry. It was often performed alone, without the rest of the ballet. There are three exquisite solos for girls – traditionally the biggest success with the Russian audiences – and the hero was given some dancing borrowed from earlier scenes. These dances had doubtless been extensively revised since Petipa's days (when the senior male dancer was usually primarily a partner), notably by the virtuoso Vachtang Chaboukiani.

When Nureyev first produced the Kingdom of the Shades scene for the Royal Ballet in 1963 he introduced a new role for British male dancers and a new style in heroes. The part of Solor, the unlucky lover, demands a combination of exotic orientalism and virtuosity which was outside the normal range of British dancers. It was one of the first vehicles in which Nureyev could display his sensational technique (held by both Karsavina and Grigoriev, Diaghilev's regisseur, to be the equal of Nijinsky's), and was to prove a formidable test piece later on for Royal Ballet interpreters.

Besides some difficult partnering, including a long duet with a floating, flying scarf, in which the harmony between Nureyev and Fonteyn was wonderfully displayed, there are two virtuoso solos. At the dress rehearsal for the London première, Nureyev (who had danced the role with huge success in Russia) performed both impeccably. But on the first night, as he swung into the circle of looping, liquid turns *en attitude* he miscalculated the size of the stage (smaller than in the Kirov theatre) and his last leap carried him out of sight into the wings. There was an instant of dismay – but he reappeared moments later, linked to Fonteyn by a long floating scarf to go through the *pas de deux* with perfect aplomb. What might have been a disaster he had turned into a triumph. Ever since, the role has given him opportunities for displaying his special blend of virtuosity, style and personality.

Photo Arks Smith

Coppélia

Of the surviving nineteenth-century classics, three were born in Paris – *La Sylphide* (though we know it now through a Danish reincarnation), *Giselle* and *Coppélia*. The first two date from the beginnings of the Romantic movement, but the last is very different. It is a frivolous piece of balletic millinery devised to delight the bourgeoisie with a display of innocent pranks and feminine charm. It epitomized the spirit of France at that time, 1870; within a few weeks of its appearance the whole society it represented lay in ruins.

There is no doubt that the ballet would have followed many like it into oblivion if it had not been for the score by Léo Delibes. This has ensured it an unlikely longevity. Its neo-rococo flavour still proves popular and has tempted many choreographers. If the coy perfumes of the Second Empire can be kept at bay, it can offer an attractive role to a soubrette ballerina and a positive, extrovert role for the leading man.

In the original production even the hero Franz was danced by a girl (*en travesti*, a favourite diversion at that time) and the role had few openings for the man. Since then it has been somewhat strengthened but is usually given to a *demi-caractère* artist who is at least as much an actor as a dancer. It is hardly surprising that Nureyev did not take it on for a long time. It was perhaps his success in the part of the young barber Basilio in *Don Quixote*, a similarly cheeky and mischievous character, which led to it.

Another strong inducement must have been the chance to play opposite Erik Bruhn, the celebrated Danish star, who was making his debut as the old toymaker Dr Coppelius in his own production for the Canadian National Ballet. With his sturdy physique and vigorous style, Nureyev makes a convincing young tearaway; the element of good-natured fun in the part reflects a side in his own character which often surfaces in rehearsal, when he loves to clown to relieve the tensions. He brings to a part which can be objectionably insensitive and aggressive a childlike charm which renders the teasing as an expression of overflowing high spirits. The vigour of his dancing infects every movement; it warms the fooling and love-making (this Franz surely has a girl in every village for miles around); it gives life to his oafish exchanges with the cleverer but slightly senile toymaker; and its vitality lends fire to the virtuosities of the big displays. A healthy animal innocence invades what can easily become a boudoir ballet.

Photo Beverley Gallegos

Le Corsaire

The glamorous east – either India (China and Japan being too distant to exert an attraction) or the far shores of the Mediterranean – was an irresistible magnet to the poets and artists of the Romantic movement. Whether in tales of chivalry and crusades (such as have survived in *Raymonda*), or in the seductive combination of sensuality and violence which started with Delacroix's paintings and flourished until *Schéhérazade* and beyond, every branch of art became saturated with oriental sex and savagery.

One of the earliest exponents of the genre was Byron. His poem *The Corsair* presented the titillating and (as virtue was finally preserved) elevating image of a delicate girl captured by a ferocious bandit. In 1837 it appeared in ballet form at the King's Theatre in London. But a second version was to have much greater success. This was arranged by Joseph Mazilier for the Paris Opéra and was launched in 1856, to enormous acclaim. The sensation it caused owed at least as much to the scenic effects – which included an impressively catastrophic shipwreck – as to the dancing; but it also provided a rich part for the Italian ballerina Carolina Rosati as the heroine Medora, and for her pirate lover Conrad. This role was allotted to a specially imported Italian mime, Domenico Segarelli, who specialized in the 'terrible, menacing' look specified in the scenario.

The ballet did not survive long in the Paris repertory, but Jules Perrot produced it in Russia and in 1868 Petipa mounted a new version to the same score, by Adam, and this was to last for many years. In the manner of the period it was revised and added to from time to time, and the 'Slave' *pas de deux* which is all that survives in the West is the work of several hands. It had originally been a *pas de trois*, but one man (the pirate Conrad) was eliminated and virtuoso steps added to the male role – particularly by Vachtang Chaboukiani in the 1930s, in order to exploit his bravura technique, and then by Nureyev.

In its present form it is a magnificent show-off piece for a dancer who excels in the Russian style – big, slow, sinewy jumps and plastic power. This was the solo which Nureyev had chosen for the students' competition in Moscow when he was twenty, to such effect that he had to repeat part of it; this was the solo which, inserted into the Kingdom of the Shades scene from *La Bayadère*, stunned the audience on his first appearance in Paris in 1961; and he chose it again to dance in America and London the following year.

In London he had already been seen in a short gala solo devised by Ashton and as a sensitive lover in *Giselle*. But his first explosive run on to the Covent Garden stage on an evening of November 1963 – pale and sinuous, his flying hair surmounted by a single feather in a gold circlet – was what stamped his special image on the public. The sense of mingled arrogance and humility as he acknowledged Fonteyn's beauty was released in a solo in which enormous twisting and rolling leaps finished in sensuously slow-springed landings. The Byronic style, with its defiant panache covering a heart bursting with romantic passion, translates the acrobatics into an exotic drama.

Photo Louis Péres

Dances at a Gathering

When Nureyev arrived in the West he was already a star, even if a young and inexperienced one. This was a great advantage to him at first; the star of a ballet stands always a little outside the rest of the company and it does not disturb if his, or her, style is rather different. Many people remarked on the fact that when he first danced with the Royal Ballet he looked decidedly un-British; some voices were raised to protest about this, even in London and New York, until Ninette de Valois – a passionate champion – pointed out that the whole point of inviting guest artists was that they should make a change from the resident team.

But as he came to take on a bigger variety of roles, a degree of integration with the Royal Ballet style became necessary. He acquired this through regular appearances in a number of parts of all kinds, from one of the men in MacMillan's *Diversions* to one of the brothers, Etiocles, in Cranko's *Antigone*. He even danced in Ashton's *Symphonic Variations*, the short abstract ballet which is preserved as the hallmark of the British style, though in this his stage presence proved hard to muffle sufficiently to blend into the anonymous team.

One of the happiest combinations of the 'regular guest artist' and the company was achieved in 1970 when Jerome Robbins arrived in London to produce his *Dances at a Gathering* for the Royal Ballet. For some years Robbins had created nothing; then, suddenly, his invention seemed to take fire. Working on a modest *pas de deux* for two of the dancers of the New York City Ballet to a piano piece by Chopin, he found himself adding and expanding until he had a whole chain of dances – a set of loosely connected solos and duets and *pas de trois* and ensembles for a group of ten dancers arranged to a selection of waltzes and mazurkas.

To write a long, plotless piece for such small groups of dancers seemed rash, and to present it to a solo piano in an opera house was courting criticism; but it worked perfectly. Wayward, relaxed and unflaggingly inventive, each of the different numbers seemed to arise straight out of some human emotion to which the music miraculously corresponded. Each dancer remained an individual, yet they were essentially part of a single group. The balance between personality and teamwork, between pure dance and expressive movement was held in a rippling current of dance which varied from comedy and high jinks to tender sentiment.

Nureyev was chosen by Robbins to open and close the work. As the first mazurka softly began he wandered on to the stage as innocent as a child on to an empty beach; then, as he paused with his back to the audience, it seemed almost that the lilting rhythm seeped into his muscles until he moved involuntarily into the wide Polish swing of the body. It gave the whole piece exactly the happy, spontaneous, inspirational send-off it needed. In the central episodes he appeared with irrepressible but gentle zest, half teasing and half teased by the girls, carried with delicious aplomb a comically competitive dance with a rival (Antony Dowell), supported a ballerina in a lyrical but strenuous *pas de deux* and followed it immediately with a bravura solo. And at the conclusion – a moment of quiet like the instant when everybody becomes aware that darkness is falling after a long summer's day – it was he who quietly walked forward, bent and touched the ground as if in thanks and respect before the final dispersal. The hint of emotional weight raised what could have been light diversion to a level where higher standards apply.

Don Quixote

Nureyev's first impact on the West was one of romantic glamour, as a proud prince or a tender and passionate lover. There was nothing false about this stage image except that it was incomplete. He is totally at home in tragedy; but his mercurial character also contains a strong element of puckish clowning. It was some years before this side of his dancing was seen in London, Paris or New York, where he tended to remain the dream-hero with soulful and suffering eyes.

But in fact already as a very young man in Russia he had danced a role which demands a sense of mischief and comedy-timing, the young barber Basilio in *Don Quixote*. It had earned him one of his biggest successes and he boldly tackled the formidable task of producing the highly complicated ballet as one of his first reconstructions. He mounted it in 1966 on the Vienna State Opera Ballet, dancing the leading role himself.

It is one of the oldest of the full-length ballets, composed by Petipa at the start of his career in Russia, in 1869. It was designed for the Moscow public and in its original form is considerably more boisterous in style than the ballets he composed for the imperial theatre in St Petersburg, for which he later produced a rather more refined version. This was further modified by various other choreographers. Nureyev took the Leningrad production as his starting-point and made his own extensive additions and alterations both to the dances and to the production.

Successful though it was, Nureyev was not satisfied with it, and he changed it considerably in subsequent versions for the Australian Ballet (in 1970), the Marseilles Ballet (in 1971) and finally a film version for the Australians in 1972. It is in this arrangement that his own performance has become most widely known.

The final version reveals Nureyev's increasing professionalism in handling large movements on the stage. The Spanish numbers for the company swirl about the huge village square (or rather circle, for it was filmed in a vast area created by the designer, Barry Kay, in an airplane hangar) forming ingenious varieties of patterns to display the characteristic steps – mostly newly invented – and the brilliant costumes. The purely classical 'dream' sequence preserves its Petipa integrity, but he added a complete episode to provide an element which seems necessary to modern taste – a touch of romance. This takes the form of a *pas de deux* in the moonlight beneath the sails of a huge windmill (soon to become the target for an attack by the crazy old Don Quixote), set to some music by the same composer, Minkus, from his ballet *La Bayadère*. In the original version the relentless succession of ensemble dances is rather meagrely interrupted by drama and comedy. Nureyev has greatly increased the proportion of both, introducing an element of the Commedia dell' Arte in which he himself is the darting, bounding, brilliant thread which runs through the whole ballet.

It is a part which gives full rein to his quicksilver vitality, humour and charm, whether he is teasing the girls or the venerable hero, playing the fool, or dazzling the onlookers by his lightning footwork. The vim and attack of his solos seems to infect the whole company, and in the celebrated *pas de deux* in the last act he gives a magnificent bravura display of classical technique. The force which normally drives his romantic passion is translated into sheer fun, and displays of fireworks to which the Kirov elegance adds an irresistible glint.

Photo Rosemary Winckley

Giselle

When *Giselle* was launched in Paris in 1841 it was seen as a vehicle for the new type of ballerina, the romantic sylph whose unattainable charms lead men to destruction. By combining the allure of a simple peasant girl in Act I with that of an ethereal sprite in Act II, and throwing in a mad scene in between, the crafty librettists had created for the heroine a role rich enough to sustain several very different interpretations, ranging from the airy lightness of the original, Carlotta Grisi, to the dramatic depth of her successor Fanny Elssler. Though the first young hero was a fine dancer, Lucien Petipa (brother of the famous choreographer), his contribution was hardly noticed. He merely provided the required masculine perfidy and lifting-power.

With the slow rise in esteem of the male dancer after the Diaghilev revolution, the balance began to be slightly corrected. It was realized that, without more attention to the character of the young girl's betrayer, the story could never seem convincing, and attempts were made to give some light and shade to the portrait of Albrecht, in most productions until then a conventional stage romantic. George Skibine, in the West, injected a vein of very sympathetic weakness and hesitation into the part and in Russia, where the emphasis was laid firmly on the narrative content, consistent psychological developments were worked out.

In any reading it is not a heroic part requiring an awesome stage presence or dramatic bravura. It was one of the first full-length roles allotted to Nureyev with the Kirov company. Bringing to it a touching melancholy and a supple style adapted to express a slightly unstable character, he made an instant success in it. He danced it in Russia, he danced it in Paris and he chose it for his debut with Fonteyn at Covent Garden in 1962.

From his first entry it was plain that something new was happening to the old role. Instead of the customary confident march down to the footlights, Nureyev – whose reputation for flaunting panache had preceded him – crept on almost surreptitiously, half hidden by his cloak, to disappear into hiding before the audience had time to raise a hand clap. When he re-emerged, his slim, vulnerable figure with its touching pretence of arrogance marked him as much a centre of pity and sympathy as Giselle herself. His love scenes were simple and devastatingly sincere; alternating moods of confidence, trust and hesitation passed over his features, while the mime movements remained clear but unfussy so that they flowed naturally into the dancing. There was no break in the current of acting and moving, no switch from one idiom to another; it was a finely nuanced performance which preserved a sense of fresh spontaneity. It was easy to understand the hero's thoughtless irresponsibility and to believe his later remorse. Fonteyn, who had never before excelled as Giselle, responded with perfect sympathy, and the famous partnership was born.

The event was not greatly celebrated. The new fluid rendering of a role often given a straightforward British flavour and the soft wide style of dancing were evidently disconcerting. Some minor changes of step and production were upsetting. Particularly startling was a piece of choreography new to Covent Garden – a series of relentlessly repeated *entrechats* performed at the command of the stern Queen of the Wilis, determined to dance him to death. Widely denounced at the time, this invention has now become a normal part of the Royal Ballet version, while his interpretation of the role – a weak character steeled by his own tragic mistake – can be traced in many subsequent renderings by other dancers.

Photo Houston Rogers

Lucifer

A revolution in the history of ballet occurred at the beginning of this century, when Isadora Duncan (with, curiously, the academically outstanding Nijinsky to back her) questioned the whole idiom of the classical *danse d'école*. The new creed was taken up in Germany and, more fruitfully, in America where Ruth St Denis and Ted Shawn organized a company and school devoted to what came to be called 'modern dance'. Among their pupils was a girl called Martha Graham. She developed into a strong dramatic dancer, a capable company organizer, an outstanding choreographer and a cogent thinker who worked out a whole new system of dance movement as logical and detailed as the theories of the great classical teachers.

A natural rivalry grew up between the two styles, which were held to be mutually exclusive. The classical technique was based on a theory of harmonious movement which can be traced back to Leonardo – symmetrical and poised, with a geometry clearly defined by an artifical 'turn-out' of the hips and a *legato* approach in which all effort must be concealed, while the introduction of the point-shoe around 1820 steered the ballerinas towards ever-increasing lightness and speed. More and more, classical ballet took to the air, with a resulting levity of tone.

The Graham technique started from a different base – the in-and-out tension and relaxation of human respiration. To this was added a renewed emphasis on gravity and the pull of the earth (often viewed symbolically), a general flexibility of spine and back and explicit display of dynamics and muscular force. The grammar of this style was developed in classes which demanded a very different (often diametrically opposite) use of the body from that taught in classical ballet training.

Almost inevitably the two styles began to borrow from each other as time went on; but the physical and emotional gulf between them remained wide. Not the least of Nureyev's achievements in dance has been to provide a bridge which seems likely to turn into a genuine and permanent bond. Acknowledged as an exceptional exponent of the classical style, he has proved adept at modern movement.

Though he had experimented in modified versions of modern dance for many years (first in van Dantzig's *Ropes of Time* for the Royal Ballet in 1970 and later with Roland Petit, Béjart, Paul Taylor and Glen Tetley) the climactic take-over of his new domain occurred in July 1975 when Martha Graham herself composed a ballet specially for him, to be performed (free of charge) for a Gala to raise money for her company. She chose the story of Lucifer – the outcast from heaven who is also the bringer of the divine light to mortals. With flying mane and Blakean torso he raged through the role, from his first appearance – stretched like Prometheus on the rock where he had fallen from the sky – to the final struggle which leaves him in a headlong flying posture, feet still beating the air. 'Graham crystallizes night,' Nureyev declared; the star from the ballet had brought his own special light and brilliance into her firmament.

He was quick to acknowledge what he got in return – a new range of movement and gesture, a fresh knowledge of his own potentialities. His powerful dynamics, lithe and plastic style and feeling for the weight as well as the lightness of dance makes him especially apt for the Graham style, and she was so pleased with the result that she immediately set about composing *The Scarlet Letter* for him. Graham's heroes have always been on an epic scale; Nureyev fits the specification.

Photo Martha Swope

Marguerite and Armand

The partnership between Nureyev and Fonteyn became famous so firmly and quickly that it is hard to imagine that it began with caution. His first regular partner in the West was Rosella Hightower (of the de Cuevas company) and it was with her that he first appeared in London. It was *Giselle* at Covent Garden in 1962 that first revealed the uncanny sympathy between Nureyev and Fonteyn – widely separated as they are by temperament, style, training, background and age. The definitive stamp on their collaboration was set by Frederick Ashton a year later in a ballet specially composed for them, *Marguerite and Armand*.

The idea of making a ballet based on *La Dame aux Camélias* had been simmering at the back of Ashton's mind for a long time. But Ashton's aim was to shed all the period and social complications and concentrate the whole tragic tale into the essential personal emotions of the two luckless victims of an ill-starred passion – the ailing and half-corrupted courtesan and the guileless, ardent young man who hopes to redeem her.

The subject seemed ideal for the sophisticated Western ballerina and the tempestuous truant from Russia, and by a lucky chance the right music presented itself. Tuning in one night to a late radio programme, Ashton found himself listening to Liszt's Piano Sonata in B minor and knew he had found what he wanted. Liszt was traditionally one of the lovers of the real-life Marguerite, and the music, with its feverish, highly romantic pulse and dying fall had all the right qualities – even a recurring stammering motif to suggest the heroine's fatal cough. Cecil Beaton, a specialist in nineteenth-century glamour, was called in as designer.

With extraordinary skill Ashton compressed the action into a set of short, highly dramatic scenes – first meeting, flight to the country, discovery by Armand's father, renunciation and return to Paris, and the final deathbed reunion. There were no set variations of more than a few bars nor (except for an awkward interlude representing the passing of time) any ensemble numbers. The vividly drawn dramatics flowed continuously in what amounted to an extended *pas de deux* only briefly interrupted for a single scene.

To make such a highly coloured story convincing, to raise it from the level of tear-jerking melodrama to a genuinely moving human tragedy, required a rare combination of intensity and sincerity from the interpreters. Ashton revealed his theatrical skills and his musical ingenuity to great effect and displayed superbly his gift for detecting and exploiting the special qualities of an artist. Fonteyn showed herself at her most touching. Charmingly pleasure-bent at the opening, tender and protective when she surrenders to real affection, her acting of the scene when she gives up her lover for the sake of his own future was faultlessly timed, her tiny faltering steps as she abandons her happiness seeming to drop on the stage like tears.

But what lent eloquence to her pathos was the force of the passion she was resisting. Ashton presented the story as a sickbed dream; it began with huge visions of Nureyev's dramatic features floating over the stage and he dominated it by a fine flourish of romantic passion, from the moment he walked on to the last despairing gesture as he knelt beside her lifeless body. Switching from humble adoration to arrogant rejection and back to remorse, he displayed a lightning range of emotions – caressing, playful and devouring, mocking, bitter, whirling across the stage to the death-chamber with cloak flying, and stricken at his beloved's death with true romantic-agony despair.

The Nutcracker

If *Swan Lake* can be considered as the poetic andante, and *The Sleeping Beauty* the triumphant finale in Tchaikovsky's symphony of ballet scores, *The Nutcracker* is the scherzo – light, wayward and charming. It is odd that it was, in fact, the last of the three to be composed; it was first performed in St Petersburg in 1892 as a follow-up to the immensely successful *Sleeping Beauty*. Taken from Dumas' dramatization of a rather rambling tale by Hoffmann about adventures in toyland, the awkward shape of the ballet prevented it from being a success; the whole story was told in the first act, the other two being merely *divertissements*. But the scintillating charm of the music, and the Christmas-tree festivities of the children at the start have proved irresistible, and it has been internationally a favourite with audiences ever since.

Serious-minded ballet lovers have tended, however, to regard it with slightly condescending indulgence. When Nureyev turned his attention to it he set out to revise this attitude. In the first place he aimed at providing a motivation which would run right through the evening (he made it a family drama in which the grown-ups are simultaneously alarming and protective) and he also wanted to transform it into a full scale vehicle for a ballerina. Above all he wished to bring out the serious merits of Tchaikovsky's score, which are often drowned in Christmas merrymaking. Alexandre Benois had noted the menace underlying much of the music (written a year before the Pathétique symphony): 'Beneath the humour of Hoffmann's tale there is a feeling of tension, a kind of delicious languor, as though the heroine, Clara, was both overjoyed and tormented by all that happens to her.'

Nureyev magnified the scale of the story, which is now seen through the wide eyes of a child rather than the indulgent quizzing of an adult, and in so doing he elevated it to opera house stature. The battle between Good and Evil (toy soldiers and mice) took on the intensity of a medieval mystery play and the big ensemble numbers, such as the Snowflakes' Dance (based on crystalline geometry rather than fluffy delicacy) had a grand style which opened out the full amplitude of the score.

As the fairy-tale prince, Nureyev built himself a role in which he could display his mastery of technique and the aristocratic classical style (no hint of an emotional relationship between the prince and the child-ballerina is allowed). But he also changed the story drastically by making the conjurer, Dr Drosselmeyer, turn into the prince. This gave him a chance to play a sharply contrasted double role, in which he appears first (and last) as a mischievous, secretly benevolent but distinctly frightening old man – bent with age and wiles, with a black patch over one eye.

After a surfeit of romantic heroes, the role was evidently a joy to Nureyev, who brought to it a very personal sense of wicked fun. He abandoned the early Victorian concept of childish innocence in favour of a more modern approach in which fear and love battle in the young mind and nursery anxieties reflect the largest issues. The total seriousness with which he tackled the story and the stress on the broad outlines of the music and its underlying mood of melancholy seem very Russian.

He created the part of the magician-prince for himself and it is full of passages designed for his own style. The glee with which Drosselmeyer wraps himself in his travelling cloak as he arrives at the children's party opens out into a radiant expansiveness as, after the romantic Snowflakes' Dance, the Prince stands poised hand in hand with the ballerina for a long, breathless moment before breaking into their swinging *pas de deux*; and as a climax he substituted athletic virtuosities in his own distinctive manner for the familiar finale duet.

Petrushka

Diaghilev's avowed aim was to achieve an amalgam in which dance, music and design should each play an equal part. He achieved this to a very high degree in the very first two ballets (apart from a Russian pot-pourri, *Le Festin*) which he mounted. *Schéhérazade* was an oriental drama in which Bakst's exotic set balanced with Rimsky-Korsakov's score to create a background for Nijinsky's voluptuous Slave. *Petrushka* set St Petersburg on the stage, with Stravinsky's startlingly vivid and daring music reflected in Alexandre Benois' evocative scene, the setting for Nijinsky's pathetic Puppet.

Dazzlingly successful at the time, neither has proved easy to revive. *Schéhérazade* still retains a popular hot-house appeal but the strong Russian tang of *Petrushka* – so irresistibly new and exciting in 1911 when it was first produced – no longer surprises, and the enigmatic nature of the ballet's message (Is the Puppet triumphant at the end, or despairing? Is the Magician wicked or merely indifferent?) is nowadays a commonplace.

But the real obstacle to effective revival lies in the central role, the Puppet originally played by Nijinsky. With hindsight it is clear that Fokine, the choreographer, sensed the dumb and helpless character hidden within Nijinsky's brilliant theatrical personality – it was to take over for ever six years later, when he was certified insane – and built the part round it. It is virtually impossible for any rational performer to imitate such an impersonation, and hard to step into a role not only unforgettably associated with its creator but also physically built round him. Nijinsky was small and stocky, with a long neck and sloping shoulders and his outline in the smock-like coat designed for him by Benois is infinitely forlorn.

His roundish features – a perfect mask on which a variety of different faces could be painted – easily took on the look of a puppet. The famous twisted mouth and uneven eyebrows on which many modern dancers model themselves was most likely a special make-up for a single photograph; in other pictures he wears the conventional round doll eyes and mouth. But clearly he had a special way of conveying physical lifelessness lit by a spark of half-human vitality.

It is a quality which might well be possessed by some humble individual in the corps de ballet; but the role also demands a strong dance technique. Not only is perfect control needed to maintain the feeling of weakness in some limbs while others are hyper-active; the actual steps are extremely tiring – hundreds of small pattering runs and jumps done at a great speed for long stretches. Moreover, the role of the Puppet is short in relation to the whole ballet; he has to make his effect strongly and quickly. It is a challenge for any dancer.

Nureyev first tackled it in the Royal Ballet's production in 1963. It was immediately apparent that he had a big physical handicap. His broad shoulders were always discernible under the white costume, and his strongly-marked features remained very visible even under the 'twisted' make-up he adopted. Mainly for this reason his first attempt was not very successful; it was tragic, but on a purely human level which conveyed much of his own character as the essential outsider.

In later interpretations with the Dutch National Ballet and the Paris Opéra Ballet he revised his interpretation to fit far better into his special physique. It is hard for him to look weak on the stage, and he under-emphasizes the pathos in the role (which can, in any case, easily degenerate into sentimentality). His Puppet is an automaton, dejectedly aware of its own nature; it is rejected, trapped and ultimately obliterated. But all the time we are aware of an obstinate spark of vitality inside it. Its spirit is indestructible. It is the symbol, not of martyrdom, but of defiant survival.

Photo Frederika Davis

The Prodigal Son

George Balanchine is without doubt the greatest of all Russian choreographers. Ironically his whole career has been in the West; he was one of the first of the dancers who, in the last forty years, have left Leningrad and not gone back.

He has become famous for his prodigious work in America, as the founder-director of the New York City Ballet and as the creator of practically all of its repertoire, which includes a number of works widely recognized as masterpieces. Most of these are abstract arrangements – constructions of pure dancing intimately linked to the music which accompanies them. It can be seen now that they form part of the same wave which carried abstract art across America (it too had started in Russia), and that they shared the slightly puritanical taste for austerity which led to Minimal Art; dance as pure movement was part of the widespread loyalty to the Thing in Itself. All outside ingredients – whether of story, mood or period decoration – were abjured.

Balanchine's mastery of this idiom has tended to obscure his achievements in the more conventional field of narrative ballet. But his first successes were in this area. Soon after he left Russia, in 1924, he joined Diaghilev's Ballets Russes and created for them a series of brilliant ballets, including *La Chatte*, *Apollo* and, in 1929, *The Prodigal Son*.

This last work is something of a maverick in Balanchine's repertoire. It represented a reaction against the neo-classicism of *Apollo* whose sweet-running Stravinsky score and Greek theme had produced a vivid announcement of the birth of Art Deco. The subject of *The Prodigal Son* was totally different, and unique in the programmes both of Diaghilev and of Balanchine. Its heavy emotional story, redolent of Jewish Old Testament history, is the antithesis of the cool and transparent lyricism of *Apollo* and was not to reappear.

The ballet itself shows signs of clashing tendencies. The Bible narrative is told in short sketches, each as sharply characterized and stylized as a cartoon in a strip. The idiom varies from scene to scene; the opening scene is pretty straightforward, the orgy in which the hero is seduced and stripped has strong elements of Central European dance-style, the voyage home is like a cabaret number and the last repentant homecoming is in the manner of a silent film melodrama.

In theory the ballet should be a failure; but in fact it has survived for nearly fifty years and is still given with success by several companies. It is fortified by a dramatic score by Prokofiev, and a striking decor by the painter Georges Rouault (not specially designed for the ballet; Diaghilev snatched a sketch from the artist's studio and adapted it). Its highpoints are a tumbling dance for the revellers at the orgy, a striking solo by the Siren with a long red train which might have been designed for Martha Graham – and the hero's persisting role.

It was originally danced by Serge Lifar, then twenty-three and at the height of his powers. His youthful athleticism was matched by a strong dramatic presence, and the part provided rich opportunities for him. The same qualities made the role an obvious one for Nureyev. He did not dance it, in fact, until 1972, but he scored an immediate success in it. His boisterous vitality at the start made him the most credible of runaways – he seemed carried off by sheer high spirits. At the orgy he became a naive simpleton, ready to join in the fun but apprehensive about the company and seduced as much by the wine as by the woman; he was clearly more bemused than besotted. In the last scene he dragged himself back into his father's bosom like a dripping dog stumbling into its kennel. Humble repentance is not a usual stance for Nureyev, but he entered into the all-powerful pull of the Jewish sense of family with total conviction.

Photo Alan Cunliffe

Raymonda

Raymonda was first performed in St Petersburg in 1898, three years after *Swan Lake*. Petipa was eighty-three when he wrote it and it harks back in many ways to the formula of his first successes – a rather disjointed narrative designed to provide a rich variety of styles and a fat role for the ballerina. It would probably have followed dozens of other similar works into obscurity if it had not been for Alexander Glazounov's sumptuous and melodious music. This extended its life through the awkward period of changing fashion into our own time when we can appreciate the gems of inimitable choreography which are embedded in the picturesque padding.

The theme represents a side of the Romantic movement which has been less exploited dramatically than the dreamy visions of *Giselle* or *Swan Lake*. It is rooted in the Romantic passion for the Middle Ages, the craze for gothic gables and the glamour of shining armour, the lure of the Crusades and the pomp of heraldry. Stylistically it has (like *The Sleeping Beauty*) much in common with Renaissance entertainment – a mixture of spectacle, vigorous drama and virtuoso dancing. It is of a more masculine type than the *ballets blancs* which are most associated with the nineteenth century. Swords flash; dark Saracen faces loom; men die, not from grief, but from wounds. We are in the world of Byron and Delacroix, not of Keats.

The ballet survived intact (though with alterations) in many companies' repertoire in Russia, including that of the Kirov. Nureyev himself danced in one of the main variations, a *pas de quatre*, in his second year with the company and this was the first piece he arranged himself after his arrival in the West; he mounted it for the little group (the others were Rosella Hightower, Sonia Arova and Erik Bruhn) formed for a few concerts in 1962. Two years later he boldly tackled the whole ballet for the Royal Ballet's touring company.

In the original version the hero, Jean de Brienne, is a colourless figure – a model of manly virtue who returns from the Crusades to claim the hand of his betrothed. His only moment of drama is when he fights the villainous Abderachman in single combat. For the rest, he had little to do except partner Raymonda; there was no development of his character and not much dancing.

Aiming as usual at giving more depth to the story, Nureyev turned the principal male characters, de Brienne and Abderachman, into the two opposite facets of the figure which haunts Raymonda's imagination on the eve of her marriage – symbols vaguely equivalent to the White and Black Swans in *Swan Lake*. Even now, the hero remains a rather two-dimensional figure, but Nureyev has added an element of light and shade to his character by giving him a complex *pas de deux* with his fiancée in which the twists and turns in the choreography – now one dominating and now the other – suggest a more involved relationship between the two than the usual formula, in which the man serves simply as the steady support round which the ballerina weaves her fanciful patterns, and contrasts vividly with the swashbuckling tournament scene and the purely classical Petipa dancing of the Vision. It seems to express not only a search for new varieties of movement but the capricious and elusive pattern of his own thinking.

Romeo and Juliet

Nureyev first established himself in ballet in romantic roles: he is one of the dance theatre's Great Lovers. It is hardly surprising that Romeo is a character he has shaped unforgettably into his own image.

Shakespeare was not the kind of dramatist many choreographers turned to in the early days of ballet. Classical myths were the accepted themes, and the nearest dance-drama came to psychological theatre was when Franz Hilferding borrowed stories from Racine and Molière in Vienna around 1750. With the dawn of the nineteenth century fashion began to change, and the first recorded attempt to turn Shakespeare's great stage romance into a ballet was in Copenhagen in 1811, devised by the Italian Galeotti with Antoine Bournonville (father of the choreographer) as Romeo.

Diaghilev took a side-glance at the plot by mounting a one-act version, with a score by Constant Lambert – later to be musical director of the Sadlers' Wells Ballet – designs by the Surrealist painters Miró and Max Ernst and a rehearsal room setting. It was not a success, and it was not until 1938 that a head-on Russian retelling of the tragic tale, to an inspired score by Prokofiev, established the subject as an ideal vehicle for dance. Even this version suffered considerable birth-pangs. The Soviet regime of that time could not accept a theme with such a 'negative' and tragic conclusion as Shakespeare (and his dramatic predecessors) had provided. Prokofiev, who had worked for many years in the West, found *Romeo and Juliet* with a happy ending a hard pill to swallow. There were complications and disputes, and finally the score was rejected.

Happily a solution was found. The Czechoslovak State Ballet in Brno was directed by Vania Psota, an ex-dancer with de Basil's Ballets Russes who was later regisseur of American Ballet Theatre. He was not disturbed by a tragic curtain and offered to mount the story as Shakespeare had written it. Prokofiev delightedly wrote a new finale, Psota both choreographed and danced the role of Romeo, and the ballet was launched – with such success that two years later the Kirov company took it into its repertory, tragic curtain and all. Lavrovsky wrote new choreography and Sergeyev (later to become director of the company) and Ulanova danced the roles of the helpless lovers. When Lavrovsky and Ulanova moved to Moscow, they took the ballet to the Bolshoi company.

There is probably no full-length ballet score so perfectly carpentered for dance as Prokofiev's music for this ballet; each dance sequence is clearly indicated. It has inspired many other choreographers to devise their own inventions to set to it and all of them bear a close resemblance; the score dictates both the structure and the mood and only the steps are left open.

It was in the version mounted for the Royal Ballet by Kenneth MacMillan in 1965 that Nureyev made his debut in the role, with Fonteyn as his Juliet. When planning – and even rehearsing – the ballet MacMillan had had two other dancers in mind; but this pair was given the opening performance, and immediately left an ineffaceable individual stamp on it.

In the play (and in Lavrovsky's original version) Romeo is rather a single-faceted figure – to fall in love, to stay in love and to die for love is his only function. Nureyev introduced, and has later developed with many details, a streak of his own character into the part which greatly enriches it. The sighing sentimentalist who usually opens the story has become a lively young spark who leads his little gang as much by his invention and intelligence as by honest virtue, and who rivals Mercutio for quick-witted mischief. His dancing in the first act is glittering and silvery; and the transformation after meeting Juliet is striking. The romanticism of his soaring leaps in the balcony scene, and the ardour with which he follows Juliet into the tomb take on a kind of golden warmth.

Photo Frederika Davis

The Sleeping Beauty

The Sleeping Beauty is a key work in Nureyev's career. It is the supreme achievement of Marius Petipa, the choreographer he most admires; it is the ultimate expression of the Kirov (St Petersburg) classical style which is the root of all his dancing; it was in this work that he electrified Paris audiences on his first appearance there with the Leningrad company in 1961 (actually at a *répétition générale* – news of the young prodigy spread like wildfire); it is the most characteristic, and in the opinion of many the most successful, of his own productions of the classics; and it is one in which he excels as a dancer.

What struck the audience on first seeing his Prince was not only the fresh new characterization, which turned the conventional hero into a radiantly youthful and sensitive aristocrat who combined elegant *hauteur* with an arrogant and almost sardonic charm, but the range and quality of his dancing. This had an intoxicating blend of apparently conflicting qualities: in the grand passages he deployed a spacious large-scaled style which suggested the full panoply of a baroque court; in the virtuoso solos he produced a dynamic drive which emerged in tigerish leaps or power-driven pirouettes finishing in a cushioned precision; and throughout he maintained meticulous attention to detail of movement and finish. Added to this was a personality with a romantic glamour which not only impressed the critics but fascinated a public outside the ballet world.

He was to repeat his success in other versions of the ballet – it was his first role (alternating with the Bluebird) with a Western company, the Grand Ballet du Marquis de Cuevas, and he danced many times in the Royal Ballet production in London and America. When it came to his own production (in 1966 in Milan) he tempered his reverence for tradition – above all for that of Petipa, who had created the original in St Petersburg in 1890 – with a characteristic flourish of personal invention.

Taking Tchaikovsky's music as the point of departure, he deliberately avoided the suggestions of revue which often creep into productions of this spectacular ballet. In place of decorative music-hall fantasy he evoked the majestic splendours of Versailles itself, with its sense of ritual, responsibilities and power. The majestic grandeur of the eighteenth century (which was echoed by the tsarist pomp of the court for whom the ballet had been written) was re-created in scenes of ceremony and stately dignity. Perrault's slightly satirical fable was approached in a spirit of total seriousness; it was turned from a fairy tale into a myth.

The result is fuller and richer than most productions. The venom of the wicked Carabosse is laced with sophisticated cruelty (her fatal weapon is a glittering pin drawn from her own headdress); the King and Queen have a quiet and compassionate authority; the court may be stuffy, but it has the dignity of tradition. Even the Fairies are aristocrats, sharply distinguished from the court entertainers.

Into this richly crusted, inflexible world the young hero strides like an outrunner from a new generation. The supercilious and fastidious princeling, toying with his attendant duchesses as carelessly as with his plumed hat and jewelled whip, turns by magic into a committed lover. The moment of metamorphosis is marked by a long and highly personal solo full of twists and pauses and wayward beats and runs which seems to reflect a turmoil of doubts and resolutions before the fateful decision is taken. Its technical difficulties are laid out in a long cadenza to carry an undulating choreographic line to an inevitable conclusion. In the same way as Ivanov's romantic interpolations into Swan Lake, it prepares us for the fireworks of the finale. The combination of the two styles reveals much about Nureyev both as a dancer and as a man.

Photo Louis Péres

Swan Lake

Of all ballets ever written, *Swan Lake* is probably the best known today. The combination of the poetic theme, the ecstatic choreography of the romantic lakeside scenes (prepared by Pepita but carried out by Ivanov) and, above all, Tchaikovsky's vibrant score have made it as popular among inexperienced viewers as with fastidious experts.

Yet it had an awkward start. The music was commissioned from Tchaikovsky by the Bolshoi Theatre in Moscow in 1875 'I need the money and I have long cherished a desire to try my hand at this type of music,' he wrote to Rimsky-Korsakov. It was launched in February 1877 but the orchestra found his score difficult and it was seriously cut and altered; the choreography, (by Julius Reisinger) was poor and the designs feeble. It was withdrawn after a few performances. A revival three years later with new choreography (by Joseph Hansen) fared no better.

But thirteen years later a new director at the Maryinsky Theatre in St Petersburg, Vsevolojsky, elated by the success of *The Sleeping Beauty* and *The Nutcracker* by the same composer, wrote off to Moscow for the abandoned score. The revival was entrusted to Petipa. The work was already in hand when Tchaikovsky died; at a memorial concert, in 1893, the second (lakeside) act was performed at a concert in his memory. The complete work was presented two years later and scored immediate success. It has remained a general favourite in Russia ever since and, though it was not popular at the start of the century, audiences in the West have since proved equally responsive. A Swan Queen in a tutu has become the accepted symbol of classical ballet.

There is no equivalent symbol for a man and the hero of the Petipa-Ivanov ballet had only a modest role as a partner and foil to the star. The Prince in that first production was Pavel Gerdt, a splendid dancer but already over fifty. The supposedly mutual romance between hero and heroine was in fact little more than a supported solo; the male role called for a noble carriage and strong arms but not much else.

The rise of the male dancer in Russia encouraged changes. Nureyev took the part of the Prince in his second year with the Kirov. The first time he danced the role in the West (with the Royal Ballet in 1962) he introduced at the end of Act I a melancholy dance of his own devising, a change which aroused a good deal of opposition but is now generally accepted.

For the rest he was happy to follow the normal lines of the ballet, whose romantic-classical style exactly fits his temperament. When he mounted his own version in Vienna in 1964, he contributed a number of new dances and formations, and used the dramatic finale of the Bourmeister production, in which the Prince is drowned beneath the waves as the evil Rothbart causes the lake to overflow. But the traditional line and character of the ballet remains untouched, while his own role of the Prince is altered only to highlight its possibilities. His courtly but reserved charm at his own birthday party; the tenderness with which he tentatively approaches the unhappy Swan Princess beside the lake; his slightly desperate encounter with the false Black Swan; and the anguished search for the loving creature he has betrayed – these add up to an exceptionally consistent and eloquent interpretation, in which intense feeling is contained in the purest classical style.

Photo Leslie E Spatt

La Sylphide

There is no living male dancer whom Nureyev has admired more than Erik Bruhn, yet few dancers are more dissimilar. While Nureyev epitomizes the best in the Russian style – open, dramatic, spacious, sculptural and flowing – Bruhn is visibly a supreme product of the Danish school, elegant, cool, quick, neat and light. He is stylistically a descendant of August Bournonville, director of the Copenhagen company – off and on – from 1829 to 1860. Bournonville's greatest ballet was *La Sylphide*.

Strictly speaking it is not his work at all; he adapted the choreography from that of Filippo Taglioni, who had written it in 1832 for his daughter, the famous Marie Taglioni. Taglioni's ethereal lightness and grace launched a whole new style of dancing and the role of the sylphide was framed to exploit her qualities. As the seductive phantom who lures away the young Scottish Highlander on the eve of his marriage, she established herself as the star of her generation and the model of generations of dancers. The 'romantic ballerina' – fey and fragile, floating mystically across the stage in a cloud of white tulle – had been born.

She symbolized an unearthly figment of the imagination, and to set her off her lover clearly had to be warm-blooded and lively. Nureyev had for long been intrigued by the technical demands of the Bournonville style, with its quicksilver beats and spring-heeled jumps. Bournonville had been a pupil of the great French virtuoso dancer Auguste Vestris, and retained many of his qualities in his teaching. Nureyev was much impressed by Bruhn's own variation on it – somewhat more open and fluent – and he admired Bournonville's Mozartian freshness of invention. He first danced a duet from *La Sylphide* at a concert with Fonteyn in 1963.

It was fascinating to watch the meeting of the two contrasting styles. Nureyev had scant knowledge of Scotland – he dispensed with the sporran when he first donned the kilt – and the style was unfamiliar to him. But the dizzy *enchaînements* of beats and turns and the lightning switches of weight and changes of direction were clearly a joy for him to perform, while the romantic attitudes required by the story came naturally to him. He fell so easily into the role that when Bruhn suffered an injury and had to cancel a performance of the full-length ballet in Toronto, he stepped in after four days' rehearsal and scored a convincing success. (Subsequently they were to have the visible enjoyment of appearing in the ballet together, with Nureyev as the young hero and Bruhn as the wicked witch who destroys his innocence.)

Since then he has danced the part with many companies and forged a personal style in it which is true both to the choreographer and to himself. He has always excelled at beaten steps – his high jump gives him time to make them cleanly and evenly – and at the sharp flourish of a *rond de jambe*; and the Scottish country dances in the first act give him the chance to release all his buoyant zest and high spirits. As a wild-eyed, besotted lover he is in his element, and to the bounding virtuoso solos he adds a plasticity of the torso combined with a virile strength which is all his own. He suggests a healthy resilience which turns his despair into a mere setback; it is hard not to believe that this bonny lad will find another girl to console him.

The Roles

Afternoon of a Faun

CHOREOGRAPHY Robbins
MUSIC Debussy
PREMIÈRE 1953
FIRST PERFORMED 1971

A modern version of the 1912 Nijinsky
ballet (with Jennifer Penney)

Photos Leslie E Spatt

Agon

CHOREOGRAPHY Balanchine
MUSIC Stravinsky
PREMIÈRE 1957
FIRST PERFORMED 1973

An abstract suite of dances

Photos Leslie E Spatt

Antigone

CHOREOGRAPHY Cranko
MUSIC Theodorakis
PREMIÈRE 1959
FIRST PERFORMED 1962

As Etiocles, one of the warring brothers
in Sophocles' tragedy (with Svetlana
Beriosova and David Drew)

Photo Ardan

Apollo

CHOREOGRAPHY Balanchine
MUSIC Stravinsky
PREMIÈRE 1928
FIRST PERFORMED 1967

The god is born and takes charge of the
Muses

Photo Vartoogian

Photo Leslie E Spatt

Photo Palffy

Photo Leslie E Spatt

Photos Leslie E Spatt

Appalachian Spring

CHOREOGRAPHY Martha Graham
MUSIC Aaron Copland
PREMIÈRE 1944
FIRST PERFORMED 1975

As the Revivalist in a dance with a
flavour of the nineteenth-century
American countryside (with
the Martha Graham Company)

Photo Vartoogian

145

Aureole

CHOREOGRAPHY Paul Taylor
MUSIC Handel
PREMIÈRE 1962
FIRST PERFORMED 1971

A lyrical abstract suite

Photo Frederika Davis

Photo Photo Pic

Photo Leslie E Spatt

Photo Zoë Dominic

Birthday Offering

CHOREOGRAPHY Ashton
MUSIC Glazounov
PREMIÈRE 1956
FIRST PERFORMED 1967

Classical suite composed for the Royal
Ballet's twenty-fifth birthday (with
Fonteyn)

Photo Ardan

154

Blown by a
Gentle Wind

CHOREOGRAPHY van Dantzig
MUSIC Richard Strauss
PREMIÈRE 1975
FIRST PERFORMED 1975

Specially created role: the hero moves
through life accompanied by two angels
(with de Roo and Pleines)

Photo Jorge Fatauros

The Bluebird

CHOREOGRAPHY Petipa
MUSIC Tchaikovsky
PREMIÈRE 1890
FIRST PERFORMED 1960

As the Bluebird in the famous *pas de deux* from *The Sleeping Beauty* (with Alla Sizova)

Photo Serge Lido

Photo Serge Lido

156

A Book of Beasts

CHOREOGRAPHY Paul Taylor
MUSIC mixed score
PREMIÈRE 1971
FIRST PERFORMED 1971

Short scenes derived from the story by
Borges (with the Paul Taylor Company)

Photo Kenn Duncan

Checkmate

CHOREOGRAPHY de Valois
MUSIC Bliss
PREMIÈRE 1937
FIRST PERFORMED 1971

As the Red Knight, in a ballet based on a
game of chess (with the Royal Ballet)

Photo Leslie E Spatt

Coppélia

CHOREOGRAPHY Saint-Léon et. al.
MUSIC Delibes
PREMIÈRE 1870
FIRST PERFORMED 1974

As Franz, who pursues his girl into the
workshop of a toymaker (Erik Bruhn)

All photos Beverley Gallegos

Photo Beverley Gallegos

Le Corsaire

CHOREOGRAPHY Petipa/Chaboukiani
MUSIC Drigo
PREMIÈRE 1868/1899
FIRST PERFORMED 1957

A *pas de deux* from the ballet based on
Byron's poem (with Fonteyn); and in a
television performance

Photo Joe Bangay

Photo Leslie E Spatt

Photo Leslie E Spatt

Photos Martha Swope

Dances at a Gathering

CHOREOGRAPHY Robbins
MUSIC Chopin
PREMIÈRE 1969
FIRST PERFORMED 1970

A suite of dances with a Polish flavour,
to waltzes and mazurkas on the piano
(with Antoinette Sibley, David Wall,
Laura Connor and Ann Jenner)

Photo Rosemary Winckley

Photo Edward Griffiths

Photo G. B. Wilson

Photo Jennie Walton

Photo G. B. Wilson

Diana and Actaeon

CHOREOGRAPHY Perrot/Chaboukiani
MUSIC Pugni
PREMIÈRE 1844/1935
FIRST PERFORMED 1957

A *pas de deux* adapted from the 1844
ballet *Esmeralda*, in rehearsal (with
Svetlana Beriosova) and in a
television performance

Divertimento

CHOREOGRAPHY MacMillan
MUSIC Bartók
PREMIÈRE 1963
FIRST PERFORMED 1963

An abstract gala *pas de deux* (with
Fonteyn)

Photo Keith Money

Don Juan

CHOREOGRAPHY John Neumeier
MUSIC Gluck/de Victoria
PREMIÈRE 1972
FIRST PERFORMED 1973

The great philanderer falls in love with
Death (with the National Ballet of
Canada)

Don Quixote

CHOREOGRAPHY Petipa/Nureyev
MUSIC Minkus
PREMIÈRE 1869
FIRST PERFORMED 1959

As the young barber Basilio in the ballet
based on Cervantes' story (with the
Kirov Ballet, page 180 *top*; and in his own
production with Lucette Aldous and the
Australian Ballet)

Photo Dina Makarova

Photo Rosemary Winckley

DON QUIXOTE

Photo Dina Makarova

Photo Rosemary Winckley

181

The Dream

CHOREOGRAPHY Ashton
MUSIC Mendelssohn
PREMIÈRE 1964
FIRST PERFORMED 1967

As Oberon in a ballet version of
Shakespeare's *Midsummer Night's
Dream*

Photo Zoë Dominic

Estasi

CHOREOGRAPHY Roland Petit
MUSIC Scriabin
PREMIÈRE 1968
FIRST PERFORMED 1968

A specially created allegorical ballet
with design by de' Chirico (with La
Scala Opera Ballet)

Photo Giancarlo Botti

183

Field Figures

CHOREOGRAPHY Glen Tetley
MUSIC Stockhausen
PREMIÈRE 1970
FIRST PERFORMED 1971

An abstract ballet to an electronic score
(with Deanne Bergsma)

La Fille mal Gardée

CHOREOGRAPHY Ashton
MUSIC Hérold/Lanchbery
PREMIÈRE 1960
FIRST PERFORMED 1973

As Colas the young farmer who wins
the girl, in a new version of the 1789
rustic ballet (with Merle Park and the
Royal Ballet)

Photo Mira

Photo Leslie E Spatt

185

Flower Festival at Genzano

CHOREOGRAPHY Bournonville
MUSIC Paulli/Helsted
PREMIÈRE 1858
FIRST PERFORMED 1961

A *pas de deux* from an old Danish full-
length ballet (with Anya Linden)

Photo Houston Rogers

Photo Vartoogian

Gayane

CHOREOGRAPHY Anisimova
MUSIC Khatchaturian
PREMIÈRE 1942
FIRST PERFORMED 1957

A *pas de deux* from a ballet set on a farm in Southern Russia (with the Kirov Ballet; and with Fonteyn)

Photo Zoë Dominic

Giselle

CHOREOGRAPHY Coralli/Perrot
MUSIC Adam
PREMIÈRE 1841
FIRST PERFORMED 1959

As Albrecht, who deceives a village girl
and is redeemed by her forgiveness;
(with Fonteyn; and with Karin Kain)

Photo Vartoogian

Photo Zoë Dominic

Photo Snowdon

Photo E Piccagliani

Hamlet

CHOREOGRAPHY Helpmann
MUSIC Tchaikovsky
PREMIÈRE 1942
FIRST PERFORMED 1963

Shakespeare's drama seen as a
psychological flashback (with Derek
Rencher)

Photo Keith Money

Photo Frederika Davis

Photo Keith Money

Photos Keith Money

Images of Love

CHOREOGRAPHY MacMillan
MUSIC Tranchell
PREMIÈRE 1964
FIRST PERFORMED 1964

A specially created role: a triangle
suggested by a Shakespeare sonnet
(with Lynn Seymour and Christopher
Gable)

Photo Houston Rogers

Photo Associated Newspapers

200

Jazz Calendar

CHOREOGRAPHY Ashton
MUSIC Rodney Bennett
PREMIÈRE 1968
FIRST PERFORMED 1968

A specially created role: one of Friday's
children, 'loving and giving' (with
Antoinette Sibley)

Photo Jennie Walton

Le Jeune Homme
et la Mort

CHOREOGRAPHY Petit
MUSIC Bach
PREMIÈRE 1946
FIRST PERFORMED 1966

As a poet who kills himself for love, to
find that his temptress is Death (with
Zizi Jeanmaire in a television film)

Photos Jurgen Vollmer

202

Laborintus

CHOREOGRAPHY Glen Tetley
MUSIC Berio
PREMIÈRE 1971
FIRST PERFORMED 1971

A specially created ballet concerned
with life as an infernal maze

Photo Mike Humphrey

Laurençia

CHOREOGRAPHY Chaboukiani
MUSIC Krein
PREMIÈRE 1939
FIRST PERFORMED 1958

The *pas de six* from a ballet with a
Spanish setting (with Svetlana
Beriosova)

The Lesson

CHOREOGRAPHY Flindt
MUSIC Delerue
PREMIÈRE 1963
FIRST PERFORMED 1975

As the sadistic dance teacher who kills
his pupils, in a ballet translation of the
play by Ionesco (with Andrea Durant)

Photo Jorge Fatauros

207

Lucifer

CHOREOGRAPHY Martha Graham
MUSIC El-Dabh
PREMIÈRE 1975
FIRST PERFORMED 1975

A specially created version of the myth
of the fallen angel (with the Martha
Graham Company)

Photo Martha Swope

Photo Martha Swope

Photo Beverley Gallegos

Photos Martha Swope

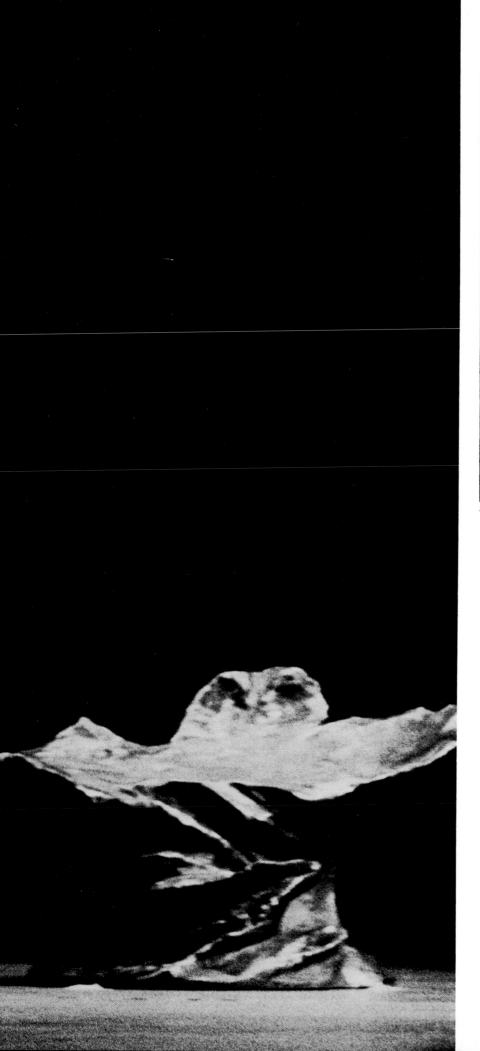

Photo Martha Swope

Manon

CHOREOGRAPHY MacMillan
MUSIC Massenet
PREMIÈRE 1974
FIRST PERFORMED 1974

As Des Grieux in a ballet version of the
novel by the Abbé Prévost

Marguerite and Armand

CHOREOGRAPHY Ashton
MUSIC Liszt
PREMIÈRE 1963
FIRST PERFORMED 1963

A specially created version of Dumas'
La Dame aux Camélias (with Fonteyn)

Photo Leslie E Spatt

Photo Mike Davis

Photos Zoë Dominic

Photo Zoë Dominic

Moment

CHOREOGRAPHY Murray Louis
MUSIC Ravel
PREMIÈRE 1975
FIRST PERFORMED 1975

An abstract suite of dances

Photos Beverley Gallegos

Monument for
a Dead Boy

CHOREOGRAPHY van Dantzig
MUSIC Boerman
PREMIÈRE 1965
FIRST PERFORMED 1968

A young man re-lives the experience of
growing up (with Benjamin Feliksdal)

The Moor's Pavane

CHOREOGRAPHY José Limon
MUSIC Purcell
PREMIÈRE 1949
FIRST PERFORMED 1972

As the hero of a ballet version of
Shakespeare's *Othello*

Night Journey

CHOREOGRAPHY Martha Graham
MUSIC William Schuman
PREMIÈRE 1947
FIRST PERFORMED 1975

As Oedipus in a dance version of the
Greek tragedy (with Diane Grey)

Photo Martha Swope

The Nutcracker

CHOREOGRAPHY Vainonen/Nureyev
MUSIC Tchaikovsky
PREMIERE 1892
FIRST PERFORMED 1957

In two studio portraits and in
the joint role of Magician and Prince
in his own version of the Maryinsky
ballet by Ivanov based on Hoffman's
Christmas story (with Merle Park and
the Royal Ballet)

Photos Houston Rogers

Photo David Daniel

Photo Houston Rogers

Photo Arks Smith

Photo Syndication International

Paquita

CHOREOGRAPHY Petipa/Nureyev
MUSIC Minkus
PREMIÈRE 1881/1964
FIRST PERFORMED 1964

An excerpt from the Spanish-flavoured
Marysinsky ballet (with Fonteyn and
dancers from the Royal Ballet)

Photo Frederika Davis

Photo Jennie Walton

Paradise Lost

CHOREOGRAPHY Petit
MUSIC Marius Constant
PREMIÈRE 1966
FIRST PERFORMED 1966

A specially created version of the Bible
story of Adam and Eve (with Fonteyn
and the Royal Ballet)

Photo Reg Wilson

Photo Zoë Dominic

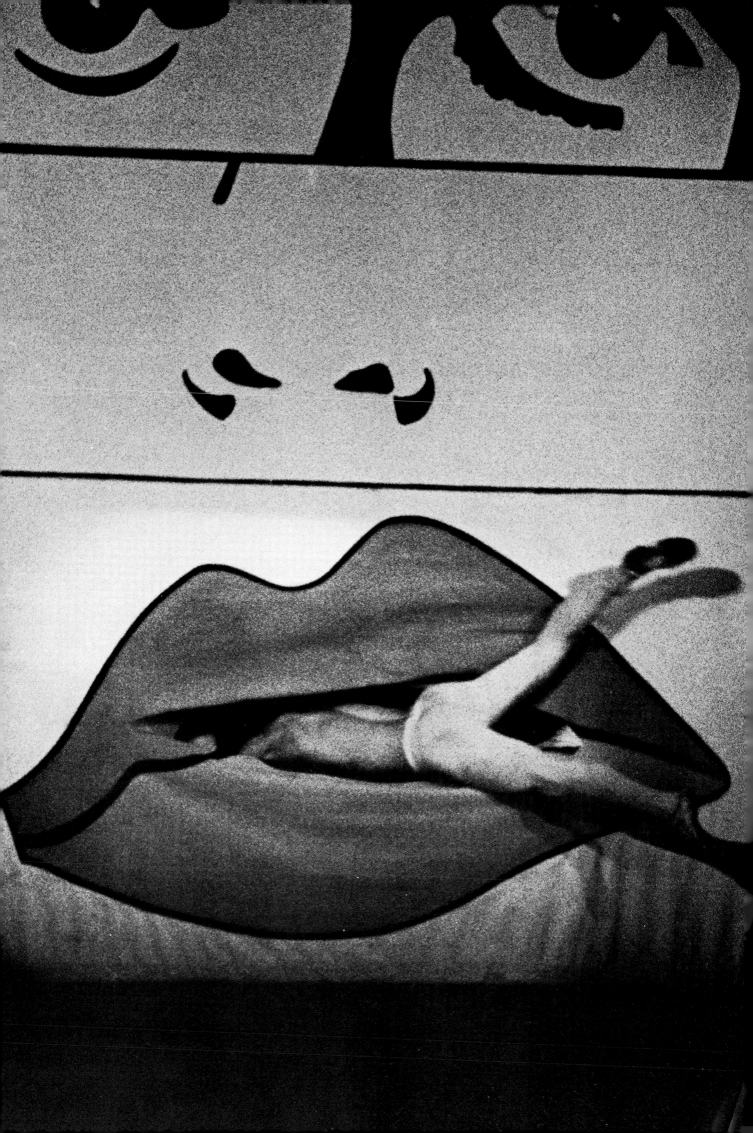

Photo Leslie E Spatt

Photo Houston Rogers

Pelléas et Mélisande

CHOREOGRAPHY Petit
MUSIC Schoenberg
PREMIÈRE 1968
FIRST PERFORMED 1968

A specially created version of the play
by Maurice Maeterlinck (with Fonteyn
and the Royal Ballet)

Photo Houston Rogers

234

Petrushka

CHOREOGRAPHY Fokine
MUSIC Stravinsky
PREMIÈRE 1911
FIRST PERFORMED 1963

As the Puppet, whose hopeless love for
a Doll ends in his murder by the rival
Moor (with Merle Park and the Royal
Ballet; and with Charles Jude and
Noelle Pontois)

Photo Rosemary Winckley

Poème Tragique

CHOREOGRAPHY Ashton
MUSIC Scriabin
PREMIÈRE 1961
FIRST PERFORMED 1961

A solo specially created for the gala in
which he made his debut in London

Photos Zoë Dominic

Prince Igor

CHOREOGRAPHY Fokine
MUSIC Borodin
PREMIÈRE 1909
FIRST PERFORMED 1962

As the Warrior Chief in the Polovtsian
Dances from the opera (with the Royal
Ballet)

Photo Frederika Davis

Photo Reg Wilson

241

Prodigal Son

CHOREOGRAPHY Balanchine
MUSIC Prokofiev
PREMIÈRE 1929
FIRST PERFORMED 1972

The Bible story told in dance

Photo Rosemary Winckley

Photo Rosemary Winckley

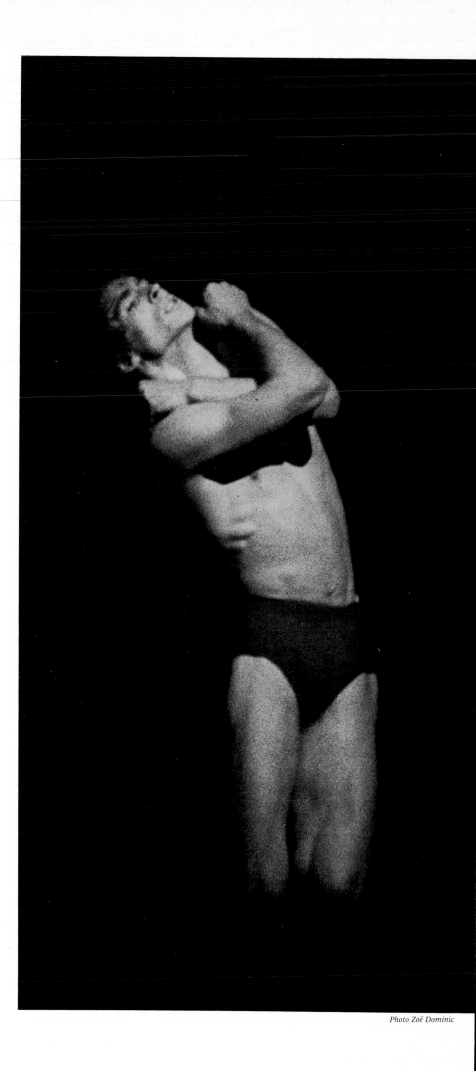

Photo Zoë Dominic

Raymonda

CHOREOGRAPHY Petipa/Nureyev
MUSIC Glazounov
PREMIÈRE 1898/1964
FIRST PERFORMED 1964

As the crusader Jean de Brienne in his
own version of Petipa's
Maryinsky ballet (with Cynthia
Gregory and American Ballet Theatre)

Photo Martha Swope

245

Photo Beverley Gallegos

Photos Beverley Gallegos

Photo Martha Swope

Les Rendezvous

CHOREOGRAPHY Ashton
MUSIC Auber
PREMIÈRE 1933
FIRST PERFORMED 1969

A lyrical suite with an early-nineteenth-century flavour (with the Royal Ballet)

Photo Zoë Dominic

Romeo and Juliet

CHOREOGRAPHY MacMillan
MUSIC Prokofiev
PREMIÈRE 1965
FIRST PERFORMED 1965

As the hero of Shakespeare's tragic love
story (with Fonteyn and the Royal
Ballet)

Photo Arks Smith

Photo Arks Smith

Ropes of Time

CHOREOGRAPHY van Dantzig
MUSIC Boerman
PREMIÈRE 1970
FIRST PERFORMED 1970

As a traveller through life in a specially
created ballet

Photo Leslie E Spatt

Le Sacre du Printemps

CHOREOGRAPHY Béjart
MUSIC Stravinsky
PREMIÈRE 1959
FIRST PERFORMED 1970

As one of the chosen victims in a
version of the ballet devised by
Nijinsky in 1913 (with the Ballet of the
20th century)

Photo Judy Cameron

Photo Kenn Duncan

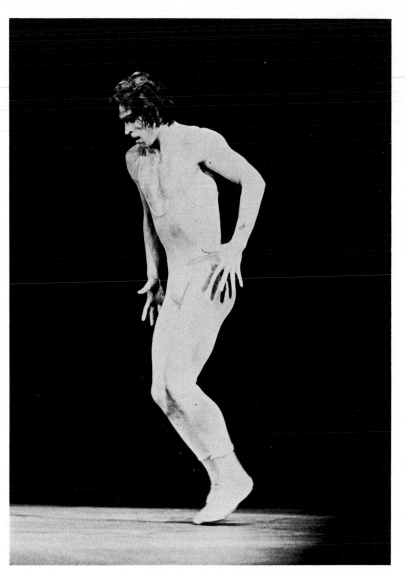

Photos Judy Cameron

The Scarlet Letter

CHOREOGRAPHY Martha Graham
MUSIC Hunter Johnson
PREMIÈRE 1976
FIRST PERFORMED 1975

A specially created role: the clergyman
hero of a dance version of Nathaniel
Hawthorne's story (with the Martha
Graham Company)

Photos Martha Swope

Sideshow

CHOREOGRAPHY MacMillan
MUSIC Stravinsky
PREMIÈRE 1971
FIRST PERFORMED 1971

A comic duet specially created for a gala
opening (with Lynn Seymour)

Photo Jennie Walton

Photo Leslie E Spatt

The Sleeping Beauty

CHOREOGRAPHY Petipa/Nureyev/et al.
MUSIC Tchaikovsky
PREMIÈRE 1890
FIRST PERFORMED 1960

As the Prince in the 1890 Maryinsky
ballet by Petipa (with Carla Fracci and
La Scala Opera Ballet; with the Festival
Ballet; with the National Ballet of Canada;
and in rehearsal with Fonteyn and the
Royal Ballet)

Photo E Piccagliani

Photo Zoë Dominic

Photo Judy Cameron

Photo Leslie E. Spatt

Sonate à Trois

CHOREOGRAPHY Béjart
MUSIC Bartók
PREMIÈRE 1957
FIRST PERFORMED 1975

As one corner of a psychological
triangle based on Sartre's play *Huis Clos*
(with the Scottish Ballet)

Photo *Jorge Fatauros*

Swan Lake

CHOREOGRAPHY
Petipa/Ivanov/Nureyev/et al.
MUSIC Tchaikovsky
PREMIÈRE 1895
FIRST PERFORMED 1964

As the Prince in the famous Maryinsky ballet of 1895 (with Fonteyn and the Vienna Opera Ballet)

Photo David Daniel

Photo Ron Protas

Photo Leslie E Spatt

Photo Fáyer

Photo Snowdon

275

La Sylphide

CHOREOGRAPHY Taglioni/Bournonville
MUSIC Løvenskjold
PREMIÈRE 1836
FIRST PERFORMED 1961

As the Scottish hero of the Romantic
ballet (with Erik Bruhn and the
National Ballet of Canada; with the
Scottish Ballet; and with Carla Fracci in a
sequence from the film *I am a Dancer*)

Photo Beverley Gallegos

Photo Judy Cameron

LA SYLPHIDE

Photo Serge Lido

Les Sylphides

CHOREOGRAPHY Fokine
MUSIC Chopin
PREMIÈRE 1909
FIRST PERFORMED 1961

As the poet who dances with his dreams
(with Yvette Chauviré)

Photo Zoë Dominic

Photo Houston Rogers

Symphonic Variations

CHOREOGRAPHY Ashton
MUSIC Franck
PREMIÈRE 1946
FIRST PERFORMED 1962

A lyrical abstract ballet for six dancers
(in rehearsal with Georgina Parkinson,
Ann Jenner and Fonteyn)

Photo Houston Rogers

Tancredi

CHOREOGRAPHY Nureyev
MUSIC Henze
PREMIÈRE 1966
FIRST PERFORMED 1966

A psychological fantasy of split
personality (with the Vienna Opera
Ballet)

Taras Bulba

CHOREOGRAPHY Fenster
MUSIC Soloviev-Sedoy
PREMIÈRE 1955
FIRST PERFORMED 1960

A ballet based on Gogol's story about the Ukraine (with the Kirov Ballet)

Photo Photo Pic

Photo Jacques Loyau

Tristan

CHOREOGRAPHY Glen Tetley
MUSIC Henze
PREMIÈRE 1974
FIRST PERFORMED 1974

A specially created modern meditation on the theme of Wagner's opera (with Carolyn Carlson)

La Ventana

CHOREOGRAPHY Bournonville
MUSIC Lumbye
PREMIÈRE 1854
FIRST PERFORMED 1976

A gala *pas de trois* (with Cynthia
Gregory and Erik Bruhn)

Photo Vartoogian

The Wayfarer
(Songs of a Wayfarer)

CHOREOGRAPHY Béjart
MUSIC Mahler
PREMIÈRE 1970
FIRST PERFORMED 1970

A specially created duet for two men,
the Wayfarer and Death, (with Paolo
Bortoluzzi)

Photo Judy Cameron

284

285

Roles

List of the ballets in which Nureyev has performed
* not illustrated

Afternoon of a Faun
Agon
Antigone
Apollo
Appalachian Spring
Aureole
Bach Fantasia
La Bayadère
Big Bertha*
Birthday Offering
Blown by a Gentle Wind
Bluebird *pas de deux*
Book of Beasts
Checkmate
Coppélia
Le Corsaire *pas de deux*
Dances at a Gathering
Diana and Actaeon *pas de deux*
Diversions*
Divertimento
Don Juan
Don Quixote
The Dream
Estasi
Fantaisie*
Field Figures
La Fille Mal Gardée
Flames of Paris *pas de deux*
Flower Festival at Genzano *pas de deux*
Fountain of Bakchissarai solo (student)*
Gayane
Giselle
Grand Pas Classique*
Hamlet
Images of Love
Jazz Calendar
Le Jeune Homme et la Mort
Laborintus
Laurençia
Legend of Love*
The Lesson
Lucifer

Manon
Marguerite and Armand
The Merry Widow*
Moment
Monument to a Dead Boy
The Moor's Pavane
Moskovsky Waltz*
Night Journey
The Nutcracker
Paquita
Paradise Lost
Pelléas et Mélisande
Petrushka
Poème Tragique
Prince Igor
The Prodigal Son
Raymonda
The Red Poppy *pas de quatre**
Les Rendezvous
Romeo and Juliet
Ropes of Time
Rosenkavalier Waltz*
Le Sacre du Printemps
The Scarlet Letter
Sideshow
The Sleeping Beauty
Sonate à Trois
Song of the Earth*
Le Spectre de la Rose*
Swan Lake
La Sylphide
Les Sylphides
Symphonic Variations
Tancredi
Taras Bulba
Theme and Variations*
Toccata and Fugue*
Tristan
Valse Volante*
La Ventana
The Wayfarer (Songs of a Wayfarer)

Dance Companies

List of the companies with which
Nureyev has performed

American Ballet Theatre
Australian Ballet
Béjart's Ballet of the 20th Century
Buffalo Niagara Frontier Ballet
Chicago Opera Ballet
Colon Theatre Ballet, Buenos Aires
Deutsche Oper Ballet, West Berlin
Dutch National Ballet
Geneva Ballet
Hamburg Staatsoper Ballet
International Ballet of the
Marquis de Cuevas
Kirov State Ballet
La Scala Opera Ballet, Milan
London Festival Ballet
Marseilles Opera Ballet
Martha Graham Company
Monte Carlo Ballet of Besobrasova
National Ballet of Canada
Norwegian Ballet
Paris Opera Ballet
Paul Taylor Dance Company
Rome Opera Ballet
Royal Ballet, London
Royal Danish Ballet
Royal Swedish Ballet
San Francisco Ballet
Scottish Ballet
Stuttgart Ballet
Vienna Opera Ballet
Western Theatre Ballet
Wisconsin Ballet
Zurich Opera Ballet

Photo Susan Cook

Productions

1963 **La Bayadére – Act III** Royal Ballet, London

1964 **Raymonda** Royal Ballet Touring Company, Spoleto
Swan Lake Vienna Opera Ballet, Vienna
Paquita – Grand Pas Gala performance, London

1965 **Laurencia – Pas de Six** Royal Ballet Gala, London
Raymonda Australian Ballet, Birmingham

1966 **Tancredi** Vienna Opera Ballet, Vienna
The Sleeping Beauty La Scala Opera Ballet, Milan
Don Quixote Vienna Opera Ballet, Vienna
Raymonda – Act III in Royal Ballet, London

1967 **The Nutcracker** Royal Swedish Ballet, Stockholm

1968 **The Nutcracker** Royal Ballet, London

1969 **The Nutcracker** La Scala Opera Ballet, Milan

1970 **Don Quixote** Australian Ballet, Adelaide

1971 **The Nutcracker** Colon Opera Ballet, Buenos Aires
Don Quixote Marseilles Opera Ballet, Marseilles

1972 **Raymonda** Zurich Opera Ballet, Zurich
The Sleeping Beauty National Ballet of Canada, Ottawa

1973 **Raymonda – Act III** Norwegian Ballet, Oslo

1974 **La Bayadère – Act III** Paris Opera Ballet, Paris

1975 **The Sleeping Beauty** London Festival Ballet, London
Raymonda American Ballet Theatre, New York

Films

1963 **An Evening with the Royal Ballet**

1966 **Romeo and Juliet** (with The Royal Ballet)
Swan Lake (with the Vienna Opera Ballet)
Le Jeune Homme et la Mort (for French television)

1972 **I am a Dancer**
Don Quixote (with the Australian Ballet; co-director)

1976 **Rudolph Valentino** (directed by Ken Russell; in preparation)